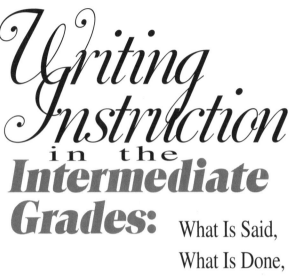

Writing Instruction in the Intermediate Grades:

What Is Said, What Is Done, What Is Understood

Robin Bright
University of Lethbridge
Lethbridge, Alberta

INTERNATIONAL
**Reading
Association**

800 Barksdale Road, PO Box 8139
Newark, Delaware 19714-8139, USA

The International Reading Association attempts, through its publications, to provide a forum for a wide spectrum of opinions on reading. This policy permits divergent viewpoints without implying the endorsement of the Association.

Director of Publications   Joan M. Irwin
Assistant Director of Publications   Wendy Lapham Russ
Associate Editor   Christian A. Kempers
Assistant Editor   Janet Parrack
Production Department Manager   Iona Sauscermen
Graphic Designer   Boni Nash
Design Consultant   Larry Husfelt
Desktop Publishing Supervisor   Wendy Mazur
Desktop Publishing   Anette Schütz-Ruff
　　　　　　　　　　　　　Cheryl Strum
Production Services Editor   David Roberts

Library of Congress Cataloging in Publication Data
　　Writing instruction in the intermediate grades: What is said, what is done, what is understood/Robin Bright.
　　　　p.　cm.
　　Includes bibliographical references and indexes.
　　1. English language—Composition and exercises—Study and teaching—United States.　2. Language experience approach in education—United States.　3. Apperception.　I. Title.
LB1576.B64　1995　95-37423
372.6'23044—dc20　CIP
ISBN 0-87207-124-3 (pbk.)

For Amy Louisa

and

Erin Mariah

Contents

Acknowledgments

In writing this book about teachers, children, and writing, I have received invaluable help from many people. My greatest debt of gratitude is owed to the other teachers and children with whom I have worked. It is through my relationship with them that I continue to learn about writing and its instruction. I am especially grateful to the teacher whose classroom and teaching practices are described in these pages: Norman Pite of Gordon Head Elementary School in Victoria, British Columbia. Norman demonstrated caring and courage by opening his classroom door so that others could benefit from his experiences and developing practices. His cooperation during the phases of my investigation and its documentation exceeded my expectations and will always be remembered. Because he allowed me to inquire about his philosophies, his instruction, and his students, other professionals will have a frame of reference through which to view their own practices. Norman is a true teacher.

I am also grateful to Alison Preece for her guidance, support, and clear thinking. Her passion for listening to children affected me and caused me to talk with children about their perceptions. I am thankful, too, to Kelly Corey for her assistance in preparing this manuscript. In addition, I wish to acknowledge the financial support received from the University of Victoria, British Columbia.

Finally, my daughter, Amy, and my husband, Glenn, deserve special mention for offering their love and unfailing support and encouragement throughout the writing and editing of this book.

Introduction

One year during the first week of school, I asked my fourth grade students to write about themselves in their journals as a way for me to get to know them better. I had done this in the past and found that, in addition to learning a few personal details about my new students, I also learned something about them as writers. To initiate the activity, I wrote a journal entry myself on chart paper, modeling this first foray into writing in our classroom. I told my students about me, my family, and some of my interests and hobbies. Every year when I used this activity, I tried to indicate that there is no right way or wrong way to do it, but I always hoped that each student would write something about him- or herself as an individual so that a written dialogue could occur between us.

One year I had two students in my class, Tommy and Susan, whose first journal-writing attempts are indicative of the range of entries I usually received at the beginning of grade four:

Tuesday 5th
Hi mi name is Tommy

Tuesday September 5th
Hi I'm Susan. I'm 9 years old and my birthday is on January 15th. I was born in Calgary. I lived there for about 1 year then moved to Fort McLeod.

We lived there for 7 years then moved hear. I' _____ knowen Amy ever scence we were 1. Our moms are very good frieds. For holidays we went to Disneyland for a weak then to Vancouver Island. In Victorya we went to sea land. It was fun. We saw star fish. They were purple and ornge. (Sorry so sloppy).

The fact that Susan wrote easily was evident not only in her journal: as the year progressed, it became apparent that she was comfortable using other forms of written expression as well. Tommy, on the other hand, struggled to formulate more than a handful of words at a time. On most days during our writing sessions, he stared at a blank page. He appeared to be more productive when he worked with a group, but while he offered ideas to his peers, rarely did he actually write.

It was primarily because of Tommy that I began to examine, in a serious way, my own instructional language during writing sessions and, more important, my students' understanding of that language. In the past when I had examined students' journal entries and other writing samples, I felt I was discovering things about them as writers. Now I realized that I was gaining only partial insight into their "inner control" (Clay, 1991)—that is, the work they did "inside their heads" as they tried to make sense of the assigned task. In hindsight, I know that the journal entries really told me very little about my students' understanding either of this particular writing task or of writing in general. I now know I did not really give Tommy an opportunity to describe for me his own thoughts *about* writing. Instead, I provided opportunities for him to write on self-selected topics, but I did not inquire about his understanding of the significance, meaning, and consequence of his writing.

The Random House Dictionary of the English Language defines "understanding" as "knowledge of or familiarity with a particular thing." While Clay (1991) and others have observed that it is impossible to have a definitive, complete description of another's knowledge processes, it may be possible to describe a student's "evident understanding" of particular aspects of writing through procedures of observation and interview. Today, I rarely miss an opportunity to talk with students about their evident understanding of writing. During writers' workshop, I still ask questions such as, "Tell me what is going to happen next in your story" and "What else are you going to say about this?" but now I also ask, "What makes writing this piece easy?" "Why do you think this piece is difficult to write?" "What makes this a good piece of writing?" and "How do you help yourself to become a better writer?" The latter set of questions potentially allows students to articulate ideas, thoughts, and feelings that may be hidden beneath the level of consciousness. Their responses sometimes indicate to themselves and to me a far richer and more complex understanding of writing than is reflected in their written products.

My own experience has led me to believe that students come to understand writing quite differently depending on how writing instruction is approached and what is communicated to them about it. At the beginning of my teaching career, I taught writing in a formulaic manner—that is, I used story starters and controlled much of the content that my students produced. I did this with the best of intentions and thought that I was facilitating the writing process by covering all the bases. Later, my emphasis during instruction was on encouraging students to select their own topics, forms, and purposes for writing. I became more comfortable responding to their writing on an individual basis, and I no longer felt an unspoken pressure to keep them all performing at similar rates. Through this journey in my own teaching I realized that, as I slowly developed a more responsive role in writing class, my students seemed to write with less difficulty and more confidence. I still could not really say, however, how my students' understanding of writing changed over the course of my own development as a teacher of writing.

I decided I needed some distance from my own teaching and experiences to further explore this relationship between instructional language and students' evident understanding of writing. This book follows the journey I took as a researcher into one special intermediate classroom where I observed students as they were learning to write. The teacher in this classroom was also a learner interested in and committed to improving his own instructional practices. Readers of this book are privy to the teacher's language in terms of how he set up writing tasks, what he said in response to students as they wrote, and what he emphasized during instruction.

In a more general way, I also describe examples of a variety of teaching styles evident in elementary classrooms I have observed throughout British Columbia and Alberta.

In addition to descriptions of the students and teacher and transcripts of the instructional language used in the classroom, I sent questionnaires home with students for their parents to complete. In the questionnaire, I requested information related to students' attitudes and behaviors regarding writing that were displayed at home. For instance, I asked parents if their child engaged in writing activities at home (not related to schoolwork) and the nature of those writing activities. (See the Appendix "Tools for Data Collection.")

As another important source of information, I relied on students' reflective accounts or interviews. I am using the phrase "reflective accounts" to mean a text produced by a student and a teacher-researcher in which the two talk about writing in response to semi-structured, open-ended questions; these accounts are discussed in more detail in Chapter 4, and the questions are outlined in the Appendix. I have found that reflective accounts, unlike forced-choice questionnaires, appear to access and make transparent students' own unconscious and inarticulated views about writing.

Our students are, after all, our chief curriculum informants and can instruct us about our teaching practices—if we let them. Their perceptions are essential to helping us come to grips with the effects of our work as teachers. Dyson and Freedman (1991) emphasize this in the following passage:

> Despite teachers' best intentions for planning productive writing activities, students may not interpret those writing opportunities as teachers have planned them. The writing opportunities seemingly available to students from a teacher's or an observer's point of view may not, in fact, be realized in students' interpretations of those events (p. 757).

Of course, it must also be acknowledged that the relationship between the instructional language in classrooms and student understanding is highly complex. I hope, though, that this book will provide at least a useful glimpse into the interrelationship among students' writing, their thinking about their writing processes, and the language of instruction. The classroom stories told within these pages may be informative for us as educators in several ways. First, they offer insight into both common and diverse patterns of understanding among children experiencing the same instructional program. Second, as teachers and researchers continue to describe aspects of the classroom context that appear beneficial to writing growth in students, new strategies for instruction may become evident. Third, insight into children's understanding of writing in school may lead teachers to examine their own instructional practices and suggest alternate or additional procedures.

Finally, it is my hope that through this book, teachers may see the value of talking and listening to children about their writing. Melissa, one of the students I observed during my research, said this about her writing: "I just find I can write a lot more if I can choose the subject and the things I want to write. Otherwise, I'm not really in the mood for writing." And if any of us were Melissa's teacher, wouldn't we learn a lot about how to support her writing by encouraging and listening to comments such as this?

Chapter 1

Learning to Write in Today's Classrooms

This chapter describes the theoretical framework surrounding writing instruction in schools today. Such a framework should help us better understand our current practices and suggest how the teaching of writing might develop in the future. In addition, the chapter will focus attention on the importance of students' perceptions of writing and their interpretations of instructional experiences. As the discussion of Susan's and Tommy's written comments quoted in the introduction indicates, much can be gained by examining the thoughts and understandings that underlie students' written words. Research shows that students' perceptions and interpretations are key to understanding the means through which learning takes place.

Without access to this kind of information, innovative strategies and techniques for teaching writing may be destined to failure.

The Process of Writing

Those of us who have been teaching for ten years or more will remember the way writing used to be taught. Until at least the mid-1970s, the field of composition was "sustained by attention to the written product and to questions about the presentation of the product" (Donovan & McClelland, 1980, p. x). In the classroom, we concentrated on teaching students the mechanics of producing a polished final piece. The rules of spelling, punctuation, and grammar were stressed, and students were often given formulas for the construction of paragraphs and longer texts such as reports, essays, and various types of narratives.

With the publication of Janet Emig's (1971) study of the composing processes of 12th graders and Donald Graves's (1975) work with 7-year-olds, researchers began focusing on writing as a process, observing "how it is done." The old emphasis on product over process began to be criticized by researchers, and professional writers began to speak out on their own creative writing processes. Murray (1991) observed that "to learn what to do next, the writer doesn't look primarily outside the piece of writing...the writer looks within the piece of writing" (p. 21). The popular author Ray Bradbury described his own writing process as involuntary and spontaneous:

> My stories have led me through my life. They shout, I follow. They run up and bite me on the leg—I respond by writing down everything that goes on during the bite. When I finish, the idea lets go, and runs off (1980, p. xii).

Recent research continues to point to a shift away from product to a focus on process in both reading and writing (Irwin & Doyle, 1992). Shanklin (1991) describes the current emphasis as a movement that is "broad and has crossed disciplines and has spanned age ranges" (p. 48).

Although acceptance of the process approach to writing is widespread, research in the area is often difficult and time consuming. It is no longer enough to evaluate a finished piece in order to discover the nature and quality of a student's writing because, as Murray (1980) points out, "Process cannot be inferred from product any more than pig can be inferred from sausage" (p. 3). In addition, the process of writing takes time, and researchers must employ ongoing, on-site procedures to allow them to watch writers at work.

Nevertheless, there is now some general agreement among researchers as to the nature of the writing process. Flower and Hayes (1981), Murray (1980), and Suhor (1984), among others, believe that most writers move through stages of prewriting, drafting, revising, editing, and publishing. Each of these steps is executed by individual writers at their own pace and in their own way. According to Berthoff (1981),

> The phases of the composing process are not distinct: they are dialectical; they are on again–off again. Revising, for instance, can, and I think should, continue right up until the last; introductions are seldom written first (p. 25).

Although the steps should not be seen as rigid, independent, and strictly linear, they do tend to take certain forms. In prewriting (sometimes also called "rehearsal"), ideas for writing are developed and organized. Drafting involves getting something down on paper—the preparation of an initial text, which is then refined by revising. Editing is the stage at which mechanics are checked and corrected, and publishing is the sharing of the work with others in some way. In some cases, certain steps might be omitted. An idea generated in prewriting may be abandoned before the drafting is complete; not all edited pieces are intended for sharing with others through publishing.

Effective Elements

While researchers caution against formulaic interpretations of the steps in the writing process for teaching, they do not suggest an approach that leaves students to their own devices. Instead, teachers are being encouraged to organize their instruction in ways that provide for the students' development of abilities in writing over time.

Writers' workshops, teacher-student writing conferences, and writing portfolios are examples of particular strategies and structures that are effective in accomplishing this goal. In addition, writing instruction today often focuses on developing the "effective elements" in writing. Frederiksen and Dominic (1981) suggest that producing and revising text is constrained by a variety of factors, including the writer's purpose for writing, the setting in which writing occurs, the time taken to write, the task requirements (stated or unstated), and the audience for whom the text is being produced. Suhor (1984), in synthesizing the work of Graves, Britton, and others, developed a writing process model in which he selected what he considered to be the most effective elements in a writer's repertoire—purpose, audience, ownership, and value. He further suggested that emphasizing such effective elements provides a less confining way of examining the writing process than does looking solely at the steps the process involves. While emphasis on each of the effective elements varies according to the teacher and the classroom, the nature and quality of students' writing can be seen to be related to them (Juliebö & Edwards, 1989).

Purpose

The research of Britton, Burgess, Martin, McLeod, and Rosen (1975) documented the functions inherent in the writing tasks assigned to a particular secondary school population. Three types of writing, each with a distinct purpose, were identified by the researchers: *transactional* writing intended to inform or persuade, *expressive* writing that relates personal experience, and *poetic* writing to create an imaginative form. Of these, transactional writing was the most common. Wason-Ellam (1987) described two general functions of writing: "writing to inform which connects writers with an audience, and writing to learn which gets writers in touch with themselves" (p. 5). Frederiksen and Dominic (1981) observed that for writing to be studied effectively, "situations would have to be viewed in relation to the purposes writers adopt as they compose" (p. 14). Finally, Walmsley (1983), in research on writing disability, suggested that proficiency in writing should be viewed in terms of the purposes underlying the text and noted that some students are unable to recognize these purposes.

In today's classrooms, teachers and students routinely set explicit purposes for writing. Children may be asked to write to authors of books they admire, and this sets a real purpose for practicing the written forms of correspondence. Topics for reports are often selected by students themselves, thereby imbuing this assignment with the purposes both of improving report-writing techniques and of learning more about a topic of interest. Often, of course, the purpose for writing is to learn a particular form or to practice certain techniques or skills.

But while the importance of setting a purpose is clearly documented in writing research, evidence exists that students may differ in their interpretations of what the actual purpose of a particular writing task is (Dyson & Freedman, 1991, p. 757). It would be useful, therefore, not only to examine the range of purposes for writing typically encountered in school but also to consider the nature of students' interpretations of those tasks. Such information can perhaps be gained most effectively by observing and talking with students as they write. My own conversations with students in grades four, five, and six are documented thoroughly in Chapter 4.

Audience

A second effective element of writing, distinct in some ways from purpose but closely related to it, is the audience for whom the writing is intended. An audience is obviously necessary if the writer hopes to communicate something, since written communication requires both writers and readers. Nonetheless, the degree of importance afforded audience varies. Murray (1980) states that "a student writer is an individual who is learning to use language to discover meaning in experience and communicate it" (p. 13), suggesting that the writer has no audience except him- or herself. Graves (1985) observed that "writing makes sense of things for oneself, and then for others" (p. 36), suggesting that an external audience does exist, although it is secondary.

The notion of *intended* audience also affects the nature of writing. Clearly, a summary of activities written for an employer would differ from a similar summary written in a letter to a family member. Britton and his associates (1975) observed that audience is a powerful motivator of student writing. They found that students in their research sample generally wrote only for the teacher, particularly for the teacher in his or her role of examiner. Langer and Applebee (1987) distinguished among four audiences for school writing: self, teacher as part of an instructional dialogue, teacher as examiner, and others.

As with purpose, researchers and teachers alike may derive insight about students' writing by focusing on their evident understanding of audience. Students' perceptions about both the value of audience and its composition undoubtedly influence the processes and products of their writing.

Ownership

The writer's sense of ownership of his or her writing has been identified as an aspect of an effective environment for teaching writing. Applebee (1991) summarized this concept as follows: "In writing, opportunities for ownership occur when topics call for students to explore their own experiences and opinions, or to elaborate upon a point of view" (p. 554). Graves (1983), referring to children between the ages of five and seven, used the term to suggest the need for students to select their own topics for writing and thus to become motivated to engage in expressive writing tasks at school.

Hudson (1986) characterized ownership of classroom writing as located along a continuum, in which control sometimes tends toward the writer and sometimes toward the constraints of the curriculum. In examining students' perceptions of writing, the researcher concluded that

> as children gain more control in the amount, content, and format of writing, they are more likely to perceive it as their own even if a teacher has made

the assignment. In other words, the more they compose, the more likely they are to assume ownership of a particular product (p. 65).

Perhaps the particular value of Hudson's work is its focus on students' perceptions of ownership as opposed to the researcher's perceptions. Hudson's attempt to access students' understanding of their own writing in relation to the concept of ownership suggests that some interesting insights can be gained through such lines of inquiry.

Value

Beach (1977) characterizes students' conceptions about the value of writing in the following way:

> Based on their school experiences, many students view writing as limited to utilitarian ends: writing to please a teacher or to pass a composition course. They often perceive little inherent value in their writing (p. 1).

Research documenting the value of writing for writers has come predominantly from professionals who have reflected on their experiences in the composing process (Collins, 1985). Bereiter and Scardamalia (1983) labeled this kind of reflection "level 1 inquiry" and suggested it is a necessary part of a comprehensive view of composition. Seldom have researchers engaged children in this type of reflective inquiry, however. One exception is the work of King (1980), whose research with eight-year-olds yielded the conclusion that some children "see little value for themselves in the task" (p. 168) and that even able writers seemed to lack motivation to write very much after the second grade. Interestingly, King's conversations with young children were not unlike the reflective accounts I gained through talking with and listening to students about writing.

Some researchers have found that an emphasis on expressive writing provides an implicit message to students that they have something worthwhile to say. Collins (1985) provided the following observation, based on an overview of research in this area: "Expressive writing may relate to students' attitudes toward writing in general and their understanding of its personal and social functions" (p. 51). Whether the writing is expressive, transactional, or poetic, however, it seems clear that the value children ascribe to their writing has a great deal to do with their motivation to write. And if children are not motivated to write, they will not become capable or fluent writers.

Moving into the Classroom

There is considerable evidence to suggest that a writer's understanding of the purpose, audience, ownership, and value of writing influences the entire composition process. And how the teacher understands writing and the implications of its instruction is certain to affect the process even further. Unfortunately, there is little information currently available for teachers about students' understanding of these aspects of writing tasks. In fact, with the popularity of instructional methods that view writing as a process, many teachers appear to some extent to be blindly following the steps of prewriting, drafting, revising, editing, and publishing in their instructional programs. By examining students' evident understandings of writing and writing instruction, we may gain some insights that will lead to improved instruction without sacrificing the many benefits of adopting a process approach.

The next three chapters describe events in one exceptional classroom where the approach to writing instruction is process oriented. By focusing on a teacher's instructional language, or *what is said* (Chapter 2), the nature of the writing produced by students, or *what is done* (Chapter 3), and the students' perceptions about writing, or *what is understood* (Chapter 4), I hope to reveal some interesting information with implications for how we may go about teaching writing in the future.

Chapter 2

What Is Said:
The Teachers' Language

The following excerpt is taken from an interview I conducted with two 11-year-old boys in early December, three months into the school year. We were talking about strategies their teacher used to help them with their writing.

Robin: Can you tell me one thing that you think your teacher does to help you write?

Steven: When he puts words up on the board and tells us just to do anything with it. Like he did before, and before we finished talking, you knew what you were going to write. And it's kind of like a mystery. You don't know what you're going to write.

Robin: Do you like that?

Steven: Yeah, it's neat.

Robin: Jack, if you could tell me one thing that your teacher does to help you in your writing, what would that be?

Jack: It's the way he says it. Like—it's kind of hard to describe—how he says it. [pause] Peaceful.

This interview and others I have conducted indicate a major factor influencing students' developing understanding of composition: their teacher's language. Oral language is the primary medium through which the business of teaching and learning is carried out in the classroom. It is considered to be an important contextual influence on learning—and specifically on learning to write. In other words, what the teacher says to set up the writing task, monitor its progress, and end the session is important to how students come to view writing and to how and what they write. In addition, the teacher's direction of and response to students during individual writing conferences affects students' understanding of the composition process. It is through language that students figure out quickly a new teacher's expectations and demands and learn of the possibilities surrounding their writing.

In what follows I describe the results of my many hours of observing and speaking with teachers who were both interested in and eager to improve the kind of writing instruction they provided for their students. One teacher, Norman, who participated in this research endeavor as a principal player, is to be respected for his courage and generosity. It is only through efforts of professionals like him that writing instruction can be examined, analyzed, and ultimately improved.

Norman's classroom was initially selected for observation because it was an upper elementary or intermediate classroom. In addition, Norman had expressed considerable interest to me in pursuing studies in writing instruction and in his students' perceptions of school-related writing tasks. It is also true that Norman was considered by his school administrator and by university faculty with whom he worked to be an effective writing instructor. In addition to working extensively in Norman's classroom, I have spent countless hours in other elementary classrooms both teaching and observing. My observations of these other classrooms, teachers, and children will also be shared to show how various teaching styles appear to affect children's writing. As might be expected, each classroom proved unique in terms of how writing was actually taught and of the instructional language the teacher used. It was interesting for me to view the subtle variations in instructional programs between classes and determine how these affected the students.

From September 1991 to the end of February 1992, I scheduled regular times for classroom observations with Norman. Much care was taken to negotiate my presence in the classroom, and Norman's personal preferences regarding the best time for observations were considered. I arranged observational periods to last from three to nine hours each week to accustom the teacher and students to my presence in their classroom. By remaining in Norman's classroom for extended periods, I hoped to develop a positive relationship with him and the students and lessen the possibility of my seeing only "showtime" performances.

I collected classroom observation data, in the form of field notes, throughout my six months in this classroom. The field notes for each observation period included information on the topic of the lesson and on the date, time, duration, and place of the observations. In my notes, I attempted to include descriptions of the teacher, students, classroom setting, and my own interactions with members of the class; accounts of particular events; and reconstruction of dialogue. During the course of the study I collected approximately 200 pages of notes.

In addition, I asked Norman to wear a portable tape recorder on a belt with an attached microphone. This allowed me to capture his instructional language and the language of the students with whom he spoke. I also carried a tape recorder in order to keep track of my own informal conversations with students. This aspect of my study lead to a few humorous moments. One student remarked to his teacher, "Are you getting ready to go undercover?" Although the recorders were awkward at first, eventually the teacher and students seemed to become comfortable with them and remarked only infrequently on their presence.

My observations in several other classrooms were less formal, and I relied more on notetaking as a means of collecting and remembering information. Nonetheless, more than 100 hours of observation time was logged in other intermediate classrooms (grades 4, 5, and 6).

At the beginning of my time in Norman's classroom, I focused on whole-group interactions to reduce a possible "halo" effect which sometimes occurs when individual students are selected from a larger group. Beginning around the third month of my observations, I focused more specifically on particular students and spoke to them informally about their writing. I conducted formal interviews with each of these 12 students during the last month of the study.

The following profiles and descriptions are provided to help those of us who teach writing to view not only *what* teachers do in their classrooms but *how* they do it. I have had the good fortune of working with numerous fine teachers of writing, but many of them have not been able to explain their successful instructional techniques to others. My purpose in sharing the intimate happenings of the classroom is to provide a mirror for teachers to see themselves, their students, their practices, and their philosophies.

One Teacher's Profile

Norman has been teaching for 24 years. He began his career as a grade 3 teacher and then went on to teach industrial education—primarily woodworking—at the junior high school level for 12 years. For the past 11 years, he has been teaching grades 5, 6, and 7. In addition, he has taught remedial language arts classes on a districtwide basis for three consecutive summers. Norman recently completed a master of education degree and taught an introductory teaching methods course at the university level. He has a keen interest in writing and writing instruction and follows developments in these areas through course work, conferences, workshops, and his own research.

Norman teaches in a large suburban elementary school that provides instruction from kindergarten through grade 7. The student body consists of approximately 560 students served by 33 teachers. To an outsider, the school appears friendly and welcoming. The staff frequently exchange professional and personal information in the staffroom and hallways. The beginning of each day is marked by schoolwide announcements and the recognition of individual student and staff birthdays.

Walking into Norman's grade 5–6 combination classroom, I found 26 students (12 boys and 14 girls). Three of the grade 6 students had been in Norman's grade 5 class the previous year. The students sat in pairs facing the front of the classroom, arranged in three main groups. The 8 sixth graders sat in the center of the classroom, and the 18 fifth graders sat in two groups on either side. The boys were seated together, as were the girls. Norman described this particular class as having students who represented a wide variety of ability levels, and this was evidenced through the diverse kinds of instruction I observed Norman using. For instance, with one student, Norman provided a spelling lesson during a writing session because the student was having trouble adding the *-ing* ending to words. But with another student, Norman suggested she read several narrative poems (and provided examples) in order to create one of her own. It seemed obvious that these students showed a broad range of needs in writing instruction. While the students did represent various socioeconomic levels, there was little evidence that their cultural backgrounds differed, and English was the first language of most students.

In an interview in mid-February, Norman discussed with me the role of the school context in writing instruction:

> We try to have a focus each year. One has been to concentrate on writing. And we've tried to do different things, but I don't know that we've done them with very much success. We tried to talk about putting together a collection of writing to go home—in newsletters, anthologies of kids' writing, that type of thing.... And I don't think we, as a school, have done a very good job of that....

Norman is a teacher with a great deal of educational and instructional experience, and he exhibited a strong commitment to improving his own instructional practices.

Instructional Language in the Classroom

No two classrooms are exactly alike, and it is unlikely that a single method of teaching writing would work for everyone. What follows, therefore, is not a description of what I view to be the "perfect" teacher language for writing instruction. Rather, this is my attempt to capture classroom scenes and several teachers' styles, Norman's in particular, to help discover individual, effective practices for the teaching of writing.

The following four major categories in Figure 1 indicate the number of instructional topics discussed by Norman and other teachers during classroom writing sessions over a five-month period. In other words, teachers addressed a number of topics (which I have called categories) throughout their instruction. These are emphasis, ownership, audience, and purpose. The categories, which do overlap, were arrived at during my processes of observation, transcription, and analysis. The visual representation shown in Figure 1 is not meant to suggest that the categories are dichotomous but rather to show a possible range of behaviors and provide an overview of the instructional language and context of the classrooms.

I will define and discuss each of these categories from the vantage point of a variety of classrooms but make specific references to Norman's classroom. I hope that this discussion will help fill a gap

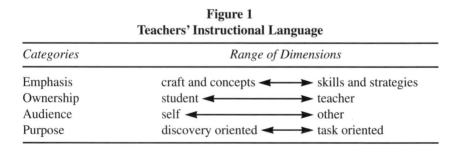

Figure 1
Teachers' Instructional Language

Categories	Range of Dimensions		
Emphasis	craft and concepts ◄──► skills and strategies		
Ownership	student ◄──► teacher		
Audience	self ◄──► other		
Purpose	discovery oriented ◄──► task oriented		

between what researchers outline about the writing process and what we, as teachers, do when implementing a process approach in the writing program.

Emphasis

In the past decade, a trend toward the teaching of writing as a process (Calkins, 1986) has received attention in language education journals, conferences, and workshops. While a number of studies offer teachers' first-hand accounts of their classroom writing programs and practices, comparatively few have examined instructional language to determine how individual teachers interpret and implement a writing-process approach in their classrooms. Through my own writing I have come to know the steps involved in the writing process, but as a teacher, it has been difficult for me to establish a classroom writing program that is true to that process. Murray (1982) observed that it is possible for writers and teachers of writing to apply various interpretations or emphases to the writing process. He noted that when the notion of writing as a process first became popular, "some people understood the process to be linear and even taught it as a production-line operation. Others...have pointed out that the process is not linear, but that a writer moves back and forth through the process" (p. 3).

In many of the classrooms I observed, the teachers characterized their approach to writing instruction as process oriented, but each maintained different methods of implementation. Through careful analysis of a single teacher's instructional language patterns, distinct instructional emphases became apparent.

Norman's classroom is characterized by established routines for writing. He spends the majority of time during writing instruction working individually with students while they write. He involves himself in their work by showing them ways to approach writing and by modeling specific strategies. Norman also writes himself during class writing times and deliberately thinks out loud about his own work so his students can see and hear his process as it unfolds. Occasionally he gets stuck while composing and admits this to his students. Then, together, they come up with possible solutions. In essence, he emphasizes writing instruction in a manner similar to Graves (1983), who describes writing and teaching as "crafting":

> A craft is a process of shaping material toward an end. There is a long, painstaking, patient process demanded to learn how to shape material to a level where it is satisfying to the person doing the crafting. Both craft processes, writing and teaching, demand constant revision, constant reseeing of what is being revealed by the information in hand; in one instance the subject of the writing, in another the person learning to write. The craftsperson is a master follower, observer, listener, waiting to catch the shape of the information.

Furthermore, Norman treats his students and their writing as being both unique and special. This was particularly evident through the amount of time he spent with each individual student. While working with a student, he would move his chair to his or her desk and give that student his undivided attention. Graves (1983) continues to describe such practices as follows:

> The craftsperson looks for differences in the material, the surprise, the explosion that will set him aback. Surprises are friends, not enemies. Surprises mean changes, whole new arrangements, new ways to revise, refocus, reshape. But the craftsperson is not in a hurry. Surprises are enemies of time constraints. Surprises are enemies of control. For when information or children present them with a surprise, the surprise has force and energy. They want the child to control, take charge of information in his writing. Their craft is to help the child to maintain control for himself. That is the craft of teaching. They stand as far back as they can observing the child's way of working, seeking the best way to help the child realize his intentions (p. 6).

When I asked Norman to characterize his writing program in an interview in mid-February, he replied, "'Writing program' is an interesting concept because it implies a package and I don't think it is. I think it's a reaction to needs." I discovered that, for Norman, students' actual writing is the fodder for writing instruction. When reacting to individual students' needs, Norman instructs according to what he knows about each student's writing and what the student says to him. At various times throughout one particular lesson, I watched as he worked with individuals and groups on subject matter for writing, word meanings, character development, spelling, theme, rhyme scheme, combining sentences, story sequence, syllabication, pronunciation, form, mood, plurals, pronouns, similes, long and short vowels, webbing, subject-verb agreement, and clarity. Instruction was tailored to individual students, and Norman responded to specific needs and interests. This is a difficult and time-consuming approach, particularly for teachers who believe that a clearly delineated sequence of skills needs to be taught and then applied to students' written products. Indeed, a highly structured, rigidly sequenced method of instruction often seems to be advocated in published materials designed to facilitate the teaching of writing.

A closer look at Norman's classroom activities disclosed several specific features about his approach to writing instruction. First, during his lessons he frequently acknowledged that writing is not easy, that it requires the writer's concentration, and that it is often a struggle. On several occasions in the fall when Norman noticed more than one or two students having difficulty with their writing, he called a small group together and worked through the task, providing personalized feedback and strategies to help students. In late October, as mentioned earlier, he provided individual instruction to a student who was having difficulty spelling words that ended in *-ing*. On one occasion in mid-November, he introduced a webbing strategy to help a group of students write a poem using the title "Storm." He wrote "Storm" on the board and had the students come up with a list of words related to that title. Norman offered support and individual instruction but did not direct students to write about specific ideas in specific ways. This type of instruction is in keeping with Graves's (1983) view of teaching writing as craft, yet it is difficult to initiate and maintain without considerable teaching experience and access to support and suggestions from other teachers who are employing similar strategies.

Second, Norman wrote with his students. He seldom asked them to engage in a particular type of writing that he had not modeled for them previously. For instance, during writing sessions featuring limericks, haiku, and poetry based on personal experience, Norman first attempted these forms, thinking aloud as he did so. He noted when a line did not sound right and when he was not satisfied with his work. In so doing, he involved himself with writing "from the inside by actually doing it" (Graves, 1991, p. 76). In the following episode from mid-November, Norman first read published examples of limericks and then had students help him write a limerick and thereby modeled the process:

Norman: What about the subject matter here? Is it very serious? [pause] It's humorous—sort of silly. Let's do one. I think if we write a poem, if we do it right now, then you'll be awake on a Monday morning. Who would like to be written about? [Most children raise their hands.] Adam. I'm going to do Adam first. *There once was a fellow named Adam* [writing on the board]. Let's do the second line. I need something that's going to rhyme with Adam that has about eight syllables.

Laurie: He got married to a perfect madam.

Norman: *He got...*[writing on the board]. Now we need a couple of short lines. They're not going to rhyme with those two. [He writes on the board as prompted by several students.] Okay. Who's got a line that rhymes with Adam? [Students offer lines.] Wait a minute. Who thinks that salmon and Adam rhyme?... Could you say it so they do rhyme? I can. *Adam saman* [laughs]. Okay, so you don't like that one.... Does the poem make any sense?

Students: No.

Norman: Not very much.

It is important to note that Norman does lead this sequence of instruction. When a new topic or form of writing was being introduced, he found it more appropriate to lead the dialogue; later, when students were well under way with their writing, he found it more advantageous to encourage his students to take a more dominant role in the conversation by prompting their participation. Norman's approach here shows clearly that teachers are constantly balancing and adapting their writing instruction in ways that help them direct, guide, and support their students.

Third, Norman responded to students by using a form of instructional scaffolding (Langer & Applebee, 1987). In the following instance from early December, Sarah asked if she could create her own title for a piece, and Norman responded, not by saying yes or no, but by asking her to reflect on the purpose of titles:

Norman: That's a good question, Sarah.... Tell me about titles and poems. [pause] Julie?

Julie: That you're to write the poem first, then you can do the title?

Norman: Yes?

Cam: What Julie said is right. Write the poem—like, have the idea and then write the poem—but if the poem doesn't turn out because the title...[inaudible].

Norman: Can you say it again please, Cam?

Cam: Well, you have an idea in your head, and you write about the poem but you don't put a title down, and then when the poem is finished, if it doesn't fit the title, then you do it.

Norman: Yeah. Quite often you will find that there have been songs that have been written or poems that have...you'll read in the book the title of the poem and then you'll see in brackets or underneath, "Originally called...," "Sometimes known as...." In other words, the poem may have more than one title. Whether the author changes his mind or the people who read it think it should have a different title, we're not quite sure. The title is often very, very important.

Norman's response to Sarah's inquiry clarified things for her but also encouraged her—and the other students—to reflect on the question she had posed. Norman also guided the students' responses so they branched out into ideas about procedure, content, and form. Such instructional strategies give students necessary support but allow control of the writing to remain in their hands. Here is another example of this strategy, in which Norman is asking his students to comment on their understanding of art in order to reflect on poetry:

Justin:	A way you express your feelings.
Norman:	A way you express your feelings. Yes?
Marie:	A way to communicate to other people who don't know your language.
Norman:	Marie, will you write that down on that piece of paper, please, and put it somewhere so we can return to that many years from now? Like, maybe next week. [laughter] No, I like that. That's going to be worth some thoughts. Yes, sir.
Mike:	Art can be a lot of things. Like there can be the art of bragging, there can be the art [inaudible], the art of making clothing.
Norman:	Okay, I think a couple of people aren't listening, but what you're saying is very, very important. So, would you listen to Diane please. Go ahead.
Diane:	Almost everything is an art that...[inaudible]. Art is in everything. Art is creation and some...[inaudible].
Norman:	Okay. Yes?
Andrea:	Art explains things words cannot.
Norman:	[pause] Put that up on the board, would you please? Yes?
Donald:	Describing words.
Norman:	Describing words. Art is describing words. Yes?
Melissa:	Art describes you.

Norman:	Art describes yourself. Yes?
Tony:	Art, instead of writing down words, you make pictures that describe words...[inaudible].
Norman:	Okay, I think we'll go back to what Diane said.... Is a person who can play a musical instrument—let's say a piano—beautifully...are they an artist?
Several students:	Yes.
Norman:	Okay. I think all of you agree a painter is an artist. Is a person who's a dancer...do we call them good artists?
Several students:	Yes.
Norman:	What about a person who's a writer, a really good writer, do we say they're very good at their art?
Amy:	Yeah.
Norman:	Good. [pause] Is poetry an art?
Several students:	Yes.
Norman:	Is writing poetry an art?
Several students:	Yes.

Norman engaged his students in discussions that encouraged them to think about their writing in new ways and to explore broad philosophical concepts. Their awareness of the art of writing was evident when they talked about how they write and how they approach writing problems, as will be shown in Chapter 4. The grade level of these students (five and six) might have allowed this type of metacognitive activity to be successful; perhaps younger students would not have responded so well in this sort of discussion of abstract notions.

Overall, Norman's approach to instruction emphasized craft, process, and philosophical concepts associated with writing. He accepted idiosyncratic approaches, responded individually to students, and, while acknowledging the difficulty of writing, made it clear that he expects students to work hard and think about their writing as existing in a context larger than school. This instructional philosophy means that Norman spends a great deal of time responding to students' individual needs and interests, and he is not always able to plan and schedule his lessons conveniently. Although his students are encouraged to expand their thinking and grow as writers, Norman's emphasis is difficult to implement and carry through within the demands of the usual school and curriculum structures.

There were also well-established routines associated with the writing sessions in many of the other classrooms where I have worked. I found many teachers who spent time planning each writing activity to ensure that their students experienced and became knowledgeable about the writing process. Large wall charts that identified the various stages of the writing process were often displayed at the front of the classroom and were referred to during instruction. Teachers vary according to the amount of instructional time spent focusing students' attention on the stages, defining specific writing behaviors to accompany each one. As such, I found some teachers whose instructional language seemed less in keeping with Graves's (1983) conception of writing and more with Brannon's (1985) observations that "many writing teachers believe that students need 'strategies' for composing, a repertory of invention heuristics and organizational structures, for instance, from which they can choose as they compose" (p. 22).

Many of us rely on a particular instructional sequence—such as prewriting, drafting, revising, editing, and publishing—when we are teaching students about writing. But when we do so, do our students learn to write, or do they learn the structures associated with learning to write? Many science teachers, for example, instruct their students about the scientific inquiry process as a series of steps to learn and follow. The question to ask here is, "Are students learning to engage in scientific inquiry, or are they learning the structures?"

Of course, we hope that students are learning both, but they are the only ones who can tell us how they make sense of our instruction.

While the teachers I observed did provide their students with strategies—and, indeed, strategy instruction is a necessary component of any writing program if students are to gain control over writing techniques—they were distinct in the ways they went about doing so. Norman, with his emphasis on writing as craft, tended to provide strategy instruction as the need arose during a writing session. Other teachers, conversely, tended to emphasize strategies and skills for each stage of the writing process, to provide their students with tools prior to their engaging in a particular writing activity. And while some teachers responded to students individually, others often relied on whole-class instruction.

Apart from instructing students *about* the stages of the writing process, I found some teachers who also indicated their order by planning methodical, step-by-step writing tasks during which all students were guided through the stages in turn. For instance, one teacher took time to plan what he hoped would be an interesting and meaningful writing activity that incorporated a long prewriting phase. He then guided students through the activity in a particular order, frequently reviewing the writing behaviors associated with each stage. When students were at the drafting stage, the teacher emphasized the need for them to get ideas down quickly without attending to spelling, punctuation, and so forth, and to double space their writing in order to make revisions easier. During revision, he asked that students improve their drafts by removing unnecessary words and making sure the writing made sense. In editing, this teacher and others emphasized a process called "cops," an acronym for capitalization, organization, punctuation, and spelling, found in many reference books and materials on teaching writing. The final stage, publishing, did not occur with every piece of writing in this classroom. When pieces were published, it usually involved students typing their drafts on a computer keyboard and printing out a final copy. This instructional approach clearly matches a particular view of writing as a process, a view possibly gained through this teacher's extensive reading of current literature in the field.

In an episode I observed in another classroom, the teacher clearly emphasized the stages of the writing process and strategies to use at each one. Throughout this episode, the teacher attempted to have her students describe what they should do during the revision and editing processes. For example, she asked, "What kinds of things can you do to make your story draft better?" Students responded with suggestions such as, "Maybe put longer sentences in" and "Check the punctuation." By carrying on this type of dialogue with her class, this teacher provided strategies for her students to use during composing and allowed them to internalize those strategies by discussing them in their own words. However, because this teacher was working with the whole class, it was difficult for individual students to comment on how they would revise their *own* writing. This teacher's instructional language tended to be general in nature, and her comments were fairly generic and applicable to most of the students' writing.

This emphasis stands in contrast to what I observed in Norman's classroom, where strategies were taught during individual conferences during which specific pieces of writing were discussed and particular needs addressed. As such, the strategies Norman taught at particular times varied from student to student. Many teachers teach the writing process as it often appears in teaching resource books and materials, providing a linear, step-by-step schema for students to follow. This approach has the distinct advantage of allowing the teacher to more easily organize instruction and ensure that requirements of the writing curriculum are being met. Different teachers, meeting school and curricula expectations and demonstrating varying levels of experience and teaching and learning styles, will go about planning and instructing writing experiences for their students differently. But what are the consequences of those different experiences on the students? It goes without saying that a somewhat formulaic approach may provide a less experienced teacher with the necessary handle on the complex process of instructing a classroom full of students in writing.

Many teachers approach the teaching of writing in a well-organized manner and hope that by doing so they will provide students with skills they will need throughout their lives. These teachers are clearly interested in helping their students view writing as purposeful and personally valuable. However, an approach to instruction that is primarily group oriented, making the focus the needs of the class as a whole, can be less helpful to individual students than another type of approach. In some classrooms where I observed, the teachers' instructional language reflected an approach to writing instruction that stressed the stages of the writing process and appropriate strategies for each stage, rather than discussing the larger purposes for writing.

Lauer (1980) states that "teaching writing as a rhetorical art neither offers a recipe for good writing, nor, at the other extreme, abandons the writer to struggle alone" (p. 54). In Norman's classroom, young writers were not provided with a recipe and often did work on their own, although he gave them considerable individual support. He also encouraged students to tell him about their writing, acting as "a backboard, sending the ball back into the student's court" (Calkins, 1986, p. 119). Additionally, Norman emphasized writing as encompassing more than just the writing tasks themselves. As teachers, we can be led to believe in the necessity of providing students with more of a recipe and stress whole-class instruction to support the stages in putting that recipe together. While students gain considerable support in using the skills and strategies necessary in writing, this type of instructional language does not often convey a sense of the larger purpose for engaging in particular writing tasks. Figure 2 shows the range of dimensions associated with instructional language as related to emphasis. Try to locate your teaching style within this range.

Figure 2
Emphasis

Craft and Concepts	*Skills and Strategies*
the purpose of writing ⟷	the process of writing
the process of writing ⟷	strategies for writing
writing as craft, art ⟷	writing as formula
individual instruction ⟷	whole-class instruction

Ownership

Ownership refers to who is actually in charge of the writing. Murray (1982) notes that although we often ask our students to write for others, "writers report they write for themselves" (p. 64). Graves (1983) uses "ownership" to mean that students select their own topics for writing, and Moffet (1981) uses the term to describe how students find their own voice in writing assignments. Applebee (1991) describes ownership in the following way:

> In writing, opportunities for ownership occur when topics call for students to explore their own experiences and opinions, or to elaborate on a point of view. In reading and literature, similar opportunities for ownership occur when students are encouraged to develop—and defend—their own interpretations, rather than being led to accept the teacher's predetermined point of view (p. 554).

My observations and conversations with Norman revealed him to be a teacher who guided his students to see themselves as capable writers, able to make judgments about their own compositions. He responded positively to students who changed the focus of a writing assignment that did not suit them, and he offered possible alternate ways of handling a writing task. For example, during a writing session in late November, he commented, "If you're finding what we're doing repetitious from last year or a little bit easy, you may request a personal assignment just for you. I talked to Melissa about doing something different, and she's going to spend her time writing a narrative poem."

While most of the writing sessions I observed focused either on a topic (such as beauty, friends, or truth) or a form (sonnets or narratives, for example), students were encouraged to develop their own method of responding to an assignment. For instance, after listening to a recording of the Simon and Garfunkel song "Sounds of Silence," Norman suggested that students "put down the title, 'Sounds of Silence,' and write down anything you can think of. Maybe even just write down some of the words that you heard.... Maybe just one phrase or just one group of words.... One little expression might strike you." Not surprisingly, the students' products from this assignment were quite varied (the range of students' writing is discussed more fully in Chapter 3). Some students wrote about a visual image elicited by the song, others listed words and phrases from the song, and still others wrote a response based on mood.

Much of the time Norman responded to his students' writing one on one. He complimented students for taking a novel approach, saying such things as, "I'm very excited about the way you responded to this. This is very difficult stuff. And I think that sometimes it's extremely difficult to write down how you feel about something, especially something as serious and as personal as this could be." It was interesting that when responding to a student's work in front of a group or the whole class, Norman did not provide such personal comments. In an interview with me, he indicated that he felt such feedback, even when positive, often intimidated the other students. Overall, Norman's instructional language was structured to encourage students to engage in various types of writing, including personal expressive forms, and to take ownership of their work. His students were often told to make and trust their own judgments.

On the other hand, teachers I observed who used a different approach worked hard to plan writing tasks that incorporated a lengthy prewriting phase (ranging from 45 minutes to several days), which students then drew upon to apply to their own writing. This instructional method is frequently suggested in resource guides. The prewriting phase of writing sessions in such classrooms often set the topic, form, length, and content of the writing to be produced. During the teachers' planning phase, they may first decide on the form of writing in which students will be engaged and then structure a writing task to give to the class.

In some classes, the planning is done almost entirely by the teacher, with little room for students to deviate from the task, either in content or form. The result is that there is little opportunity for students to direct their own writing by selecting topics or displaying their individual approaches to writing on an assigned topic. This may be a direct result of the teacher's own long- and short-range plans and goals and of the administrator's expectations. Nonetheless, it is important to note that some teachers plan writing activities without taking into consideration students' own writing abilities.

In those classrooms where teachers incorporated a lengthy prewriting component into their daily plans, I found it interesting to note that even with extended attention to a prewriting phase, before students began these assignments, they asked questions such as, "How long should it be?" "How do I start?" "Do I handwrite?" "How many events do I write?" and "Do we have to memorize it?" While these questions appeared to be part of a ritualized behavior, the combination of student questions and teacher responses often served to set further parameters for the writing task. In my experience, teachers responded the way many of us do: by acknowledging a student's inquiry or comment and giving a specific answer to guide the student with the writing task at hand.

Another feature of classroom language as it relates to ownership is the use of questions when responding to students who say, "I don't know what to put next." How many of us have been asked this same kind of question by students who were writing or thinking about writing? As a writing teacher, I have often asked myself when I should intervene and when I should prompt. What are the hidden results of my decision to do one or the other? In my own practice, I try to get as much from the student as possible before I take an active role in guiding his or her writing. Each student requires somewhat different instruction from me and needs a different amount of guidance. Figuring out what type of instruction to provide occupies much of my planning and time. When students request help, some teachers use a question-asking strategy to help them focus their writing and get going with it. For instance, they may ask students questions such as, "What will happen next in your story?" "What kind of ending do you have in mind?" and "Is there enough description of the setting for your readers? But the use of this strategy means that the teacher is often responsible for most of the dialogue and thereby perhaps provides support at the expense of student ownership. That is, the teacher responds by supplying ideas through a question-asking strategy, particularly when students seem uncertain or blank as they write.

Of course, the *nature* of the questions asked during such exchanges also influences their effect on the issue of ownership. For example, some teachers may ask questions that are less specific—such as, "What do you want to say?"—while other teachers may ask more specific questions. Perhaps this difference in questioning between teachers can be attributed to the teachers' simply providing encouragement best fitting the age and experience of their students.

Whatever the reason for the differences, the effect of teachers' instructional language on students' ownership of their writing (that is, how students feel about the writing they have produced) appears to have been considerable in the classes I observed (this is discussed further in Chapter 4). Norman's language emphasized that writers are in charge of their writing. Students made decisions about content, form, and length. Norman encouraged his students to change tasks to meet their needs and interests and responded positively when they did so. He withheld compliments, evaluations, and assessments during whole-group instruction and encouraged students to become critical readers of their own writing. In contrast, other teachers I observed articulated the necessity of well-planned writing activities, as mentioned. Consequently, decisions regarding content, form, and length were often predetermined by them, and they thereby took ownership of certain aspects of their students' writing. In responding to student queries, for example, if a teacher asked specific content questions, he or she may have pulled the writers toward the teacher's view of the writing task. Figure 3 provides a visual representation of teachers' language as it relates to ownership and indicates that ownership can be seen to fall on a range between student and teacher involvement. Once again, attempt to place yourself within this range considering the many writing activities available in your classroom.

Figure 3
Ownership

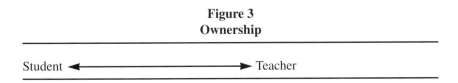

Student ⟵—————————————⟶ Teacher

Audience

Cambourne (1988) states that writing encapsulates reading. In this sense, audience can be seen to involve the writer's adjusting his or her language according to the characteristics of the intended readership of a particular piece. The audience can be as close as the writer him- or herself (the "internal" audience) or any individual or group outside the writer (the "external" audience), including groups that may be vague, distant, unseen, or unknown. Murray (1991) observed that many established and successful writers engage in writing for themselves first and then for a small group of intimates. He cites Rebecca West's comment that "writers write for themselves and not for their readers, and that art has nothing to do with communication between person and person, only with communication between different parts of a person's mind" (p. 164). Others have argued that a sense of audience as "other," imagined or real, is important for the meaning both writers and readers derive from the activity of writing (Frederiksen & Dominic, 1981).

As with emphasis and ownership, the teachers I spoke with for my research discussed the role of audience with their students in different ways. In Norman's classroom, "audience knowledge" was not central to the assigned writing tasks, the way it often is when students are engaged in persuasive, regulative, or communicative writing (Tierney & Shanahan, 1991). The influential factor of form clearly affects the nature of the audience for student writing. Norman directed students to focus on the inner audience of self during writing. He appeared to be influenced by Brannon's (1985) belief that "the dominant motive for writing is self-expression; communicative and aesthetic abilities depend on the nurturing of the expressive capacity" (p. 19).

In addition, Norman asked students to be sensitive if they wrote about one another in their compositions. They were required to get permission from a classmate if they wished to use that person in their writing. This encouraging of students to be sensitive to one another as writers and subjects of writing appeared to be aimed at maintaining a comfortable and nonthreatening classroom environment. The following comments Norman made to the class in mid-November, during the previously described lesson on limericks, indicate this emphasis:

> This is what I'd like you to do. You must not be rude to anybody as you write your limericks. What about the subject matter here? Is it very serious? [pause] It's humorous, sort of silly.... That's probably quite typical of limericks—that they're not going to make too much sense, that they're a little bit ridiculous, somewhat insulting, and yet not enough that anybody's going to be upset.

Norman also attempted to have students look at and comment on the content and quality of their own writing, as this dialogue from early December shows.

Norman: Tell me what you've done here.

Caroline: I sort of made it so that this [part] would be on the same page and it would change the reader's mood.

Norman: Good for you.

Caroline: So it would all be sad and heavy.

Norman: Ah! That's a good idea. I like that.

Caroline: It sort of changes from sort of a sad scene to all of a sudden to a lighter scene. And...I'm bringing them back down, a change of mood.

Norman: Good for you. [continues reading] Umm.... This is very clever, this is very clever. Good for you. I like this one, and I think that your idea here is good. You know what sometimes authors do, is they'll do that in a poem. They'll have a mood change like that in a single poem.

In this case, Caroline came to the conference aware of her own use of mood change in a piece of writing. Nevertheless, Norman played a role by complimenting her on this awareness. He provided an evaluative comment and reinforced her use of language by telling her that other authors use similar methods. However, he assumed a more directive role with Joshua, who was frustrated by his inability to think of a word to rhyme with "friend."

Joshua: I can't get anything to rhyme with what I want to do.

Norman: Okay, tell me the list of words you want to write down. What are the words that you want to talk about?

Joshua: [inaudible]

Norman: Okay, give me some words that you want to...that you're thinking about putting in the sentence.

Joshua: [pause]

Norman: Give me a line that you want me to come up with a rhyme for you.

Joshua: "I was playing with my friend."

Norman: "I was playing with my friend." Okay, let's write that down. Now, what do you want to happen?

During these two writing conferences, Norman assumed an active and responsive role and listened to what his students said. Although he did not refer explicitly to Caroline and Joshua as the primary audience for their own writing, he helped them remain in control of the process by having them reflect on their writing as readers. In the second case, Norman refocused Joshua's attention toward the content of his piece, which was, at this point, not well developed. Norman asked Joshua what he wanted to have happen. In this way, Norman's questioning strategy focused on teaching the writer, not the writing. Calkins (1986) observed that "if a piece of writing gets better but the writer has learned nothing that will help him or her another day on another piece, then the conference was a waste of everyone's time" (p. 120).

In other instances, Norman seemed to sense when students were struggling with their writing. Rather than indicate to students that he could fix their work, he acknowledged *their* responses to their writing with phrases such as, "You're not very happy with this, are you?" He also focused students' attention on their effective use of language, as in this comment recorded in early December: "See, you've done it here without even thinking. You've left out the verb 'was,' right? We should say, 'On her face never was a frown,' but you have done something else to keep the syllables down. You left that out."

Apart from Norman's emphasizing the writer as his or her own audience through his encouraging students to serve as readers of their own work, it appeared that he, as teacher, was also an important audience for his students' writing. During a session on evaluation in mid-November, Norman told his students they needed to be aware of his expectations:

> Does anybody know what I mean by presentation? [pause] Julie, if you...at Christmas time, if you were to receive a Barbie doll and somebody said it was outside, and you went outside and this Barbie doll was in a package lying in the road...all covered in mud and dirt—would you like that as much as if the same Barbie doll was all wrapped up under the Christmas tree, by the nice warm fire?... Pretty obvious, isn't it? It's the same with your work. Your work may be really, really good, but if it's not...if it doesn't look good on the page and I don't feel good about reading it, then it's difficult for me to get at the message. So, I think it's especially important that you want to present your work well. You want to give it—not as a present—but you want to present it well. You want to show it off well. So, that's what I mean by presentation. And that includes your handwriting...organization of the page, how the whole book looks, that type of thing.

It is important to stress that in these remarks, Norman was concerned about presentation of writing and not quality of content, which, for the most part, he encouraged students to judge for themselves. But this excerpt does indicate that Norman presented himself as an important external audience in matters of neatness and handwriting.

It is more common in some classrooms for the role of audience in writing to be discussed explicitly. For instance, many teachers indicate to the students that they will be reading their writing aloud during special events or schoolwide assemblies. In this way, students clearly are aware of the function and audience associated with their writing. One teacher indicated the role of audience as follows.

I'm just going to remind you that we have an assembly on Tuesday, and at that assembly we're going to be sharing individually some of the things we've written....You'll be reading what you've written—one of the pieces that you've just written.... But before you read it, I think we should really concentrate on revising and editing it so we make sure that when we read it in the assembly, everybody listening understands what you want them to.

Some teachers I observed spent considerable instructional time emphasizing to their students that their writing would have an external audience. Making students aware of the role of others is not always an easy task to accomplish in school, particularly in writing tasks. One way in which I observed how this could be accomplished was when students were encouraged to work with partners when writing. One of the strategies used frequently was to have students read their writing aloud to a partner, with the partner following the text with pencil in hand, ready to make changes when deemed necessary by the pair. Peers had a major role to play during writing sessions. On many occasions I observed, students were asked to work with a partner or the teacher and to follow a procedure of reading their work aloud and making changes in the text.

Another way teachers help their students become aware of audience in writing is to encourage students to be critical readers of their own writing. As I noted in my research, this appeared to be a more or less successful task depending on the age of the students, with younger students less able to see and make changes to their writing and older students somewhat more able to do so.

A third way teachers encourage students to increase their own awareness of audience is to have them engage primarily in types of transactional writing designed to summarize and report information. This form of writing by its very nature requires attention to an external audience. In this instance and others, audience is presented as an integral consideration during the actual drafting process. In other words, students are encouraged to reshape their writing with an eye toward their supposed audience.

Interestingly, there were several instances in the writing sessions I observed when teachers indicated to their students that certain decisions were up to the writer, not the audience. These were generally matters of style, as indicated in the following comment made by a teacher to a student: "You might want to think about taking those words out. You don't have to, but just read it with them in and with them out, okay?" In other words, when modeling the revision process for students, some teachers indicated that a wording change suggested by a partner might sound better, but that it was always up to the author to decide whether the change would actually be made. In matters of style, it seemed that teachers I observed did emphasize inner audience to their students.

Essentially, there appeared to be two distinct ways in which teachers addressed audience with their students in the classes I observed. On the one hand, some teachers talked about audience to the whole class at the beginning of a writing session and tended to suggest that audience is important to keep in mind when shaping written products. While they encouraged students to become attentive readers of their own writing, they focused attention on audience as someone other than the writer, except in matters of style. On the other hand, Norman and some of the other teachers I observed encouraged their students to be sensitive to their audience but stressed that they themselves were readers of their own writing. They taught awareness of inner audience, but in matters of presentation, these teachers emphasized outer audience to their students. Figure 4, at the top of page 42, gives a graphic representation of the range between these two instructional styles in terms of the instructional language they directed toward considerations of audience. As a teacher of writing, do you have a sense where you would place your teaching practices with regards to the role of audience in your students' writing?

Purpose

Why write? It seems apparent that writing serves the purpose of communicating meaning in a permanent sense either to ourselves or to others. It may be less apparent that writing also serves as "(1) a means of ordering and creating worlds, (2) a mechanism for bringing conscious awareness to that which was previously unconscious, and (3) a method for developing the language skills which both empow-

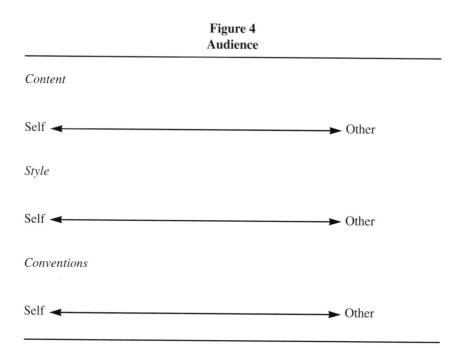

Figure 4
Audience

Content

Self ⟵————————————————⟶ Other

Style

Self ⟵————————————————⟶ Other

Conventions

Self ⟵————————————————⟶ Other

er and dignify" (Cambourne, 1988, p. 185). One of the most difficult tasks I have faced as a teacher of writing is describing the purpose of particular assignments to my students in a way that shows clearly their relevance and importance.

The following discussion examines teachers' instructional language as it relates to the purposes for writing. At the outset, I would like to note that many teachers I have observed planned writing activities that appeared to serve some of the previously mentioned purposes, and they articulated awareness of these purposes for writing in interviews. However, they did not consistently express to their students the purposes they had in mind for specific writing tasks. I will describe how Norman approached defining a sense of purpose in his writing classroom and then examine other classrooms and teaching practices in an attempt to provide a wide variety of ways in which teachers approach this concept. It is left to the individual reader to identify his or her own approaches and determine which practices appear to be more successful than others.

Throughout my time in his classroom, Norman emphasized five major purposes for engaging in writing:

- to discover one's own thoughts, ideas, and feelings;
- for personal expression;
- for enjoyment;
- to communicate using a particular form; and
- to prepare for future school experiences.

Writing as a method for *discovery* was a dominant dimension of purpose as expressed in Norman's instructional language. I recorded several instances when Norman asked students to use writing to find out what they knew or thought about a topic or question. For example, in an introductory writing session on poetry in early November, Norman asked his students to write several lines describing their understanding of poetry. He indicated that students should write their personal interpretations, and acknowledged the task to be one that he had struggled with himself:

> What I'm asking for is just to give me a definition. Poetry is...a bunch of words on a page. That's a one-liner. Poetry is?... Poetry is...[pause] something I don't like very much. Those are all called one-liners. They're not related to the previous thing. So, you can just do a series of those.... You could write a paragraph on what you think it is.... But I'd like you to spend about ten minutes writing down what you think poetry is, because I'm not sure that I know. I'm not entirely convinced that I could write down a definition, but I would like you to explore that.

The students offered a number of alternate responses to the question, "What is poetry?" Norman accepted their responses positively and viewed the session as having provided students with an opportunity to identify for themselves thoughts and ideas about poetry. In addition, the session communicated to him the students' prior knowledge about the subject.

Following the discussion comparing a writer's craft to that of an artist (see pages 26–27), Norman asked students to comment in writing on whether they thought poetry was an art requiring natural ability or the result of persistence and hard work. Once again, the teacher acknowledged that this was an issue to be considered and encouraged students to "play around with these questions." In so doing, he focused the students' attention on a general purpose for writing beyond the immediate task. This provided the students with an opportunity to use writing as a means of organizing thoughts and ideas and, perhaps more important, of bringing those thoughts and ideas to conscious awareness. It meant, of course, that the writers and the teacher could not be certain what would be expressed until it was written, mirroring the adage that one cannot know what one thinks until one hears what one has said.

A second purpose for writing in Norman's classroom was *personal expression*. In early December, Norman told a student a personal story about a friend who nursed a sick bird back to health and then lost the bird in an accident. On this and several other occasions, Norman talked about writing as a means of expressing one's personal views and feelings.

Norman: A friend of mine's daughter who is about 25 works as a veterinarian's assistant...and being a veterinarian's assistant, she has some unpleasant things to do, one of them having to do with, as the expression goes, "putting animals down," which means they are too sick to live, they end up....

Matthew: Putting them to sleep.

Norman: "Putting them to sleep." That's the expression, isn't it? And she does this—she's been doing this for three or four years. And out back where they worked last summer, they noticed there was a little tree, a little nest in a small tree out behind. And they watched the sparrows raising a number of young birds. And...they noticed that one bird was a little different from the others. I guess they were looking out the window and watching these birds. And eventually they noticed this bird on the ground, so they went out and looked at it. And they noticed that its wing had been badly....

Now I know this person...and I want to write the poem to her. I don't know if I'm going to talk to Leslie or not, but I'm going to be thinking of her as I write that poem. And [pause] umm...I don't quite know.... I'm not trying to make her feel better because that's not the point. I think that what happened to her was a really interesting thing, and, sad as it was, I just want to record that.... So, I'm not sure where I'm going to go with this....

This excerpt illustrates that Norman invested a degree of personal energy in the writing session by describing to his students an incident that was important and meaningful to him. By including specific details of the event, Norman created a quiet, serious mood, and his students listened intently. As he spoke about the purpose for engaging in this writing task, he mentioned his audience, Leslie, to whom the poem would be given. Additionally, he noted that his real purpose for writing this piece was to record an event that had affected him personally, and that by writing about it, he would be provided with the opportunity to express personal feelings. A sense that writing can be used to discover the nature of feelings was also present in Norman's comment, "I'm not sure where I'm going to go with this." Norman worked on this poem for two months and eventually published his work by showing it to his students and giving it to the friend for whom it was written.

On other occasions, Norman played recorded music that the students listened and responded to in a personal manner, as shown in the following episode.

Norman: [to the class] You should tell me a little bit about the mood of the song, how it makes you feel, [the] type of...singing in there. Was it angry, was it sad, was it happy, was it silly, was it light, light-hearted or the opposite of light-hearted, we could say heavy?... Those kind of things I think all of you could pick up a little bit. Jeffrey, you can do this. Good for you! Excellent....

[The students begin talking to one another. The teacher stops and talks to individuals or groups of children.]

Norman:	What do you think the theme of this is?
Laurie:	Kind of...like happiness and sadness and [inaudible] in between.
Norman:	Okay, and was it going from one to the other or was it just sort of....
Jeffrey:	[inaudible]
Norman:	Yeah, keep going.
Jeffrey:	It was sort of...peaceful.
Norman:	Peaceful. Very good. That's a nice word. What do you think? [turning to another student]
Steven:	I think it's just telling you're lonely by yourself in the silence.
Norman:	That's very nice. I like that. You're lonely by yourself in the silence. Why don't you write those exact words down. Good, that's a start....

Here Norman provided an opportunity for students to respond to a piece of music in any manner they wished, but he emphasized a personal response. Recognizing that this sort of writing might be difficult for some students, he followed the lesson up with an acknowledgment of the difficulty of the task and reinforced the purpose of writing for personal expression.

Writing was also discussed by Norman as an activity that writers engage in for pure and simple *enjoyment*. This purpose was frequently mentioned when students were involved in writing limericks. The following two comments characterize Norman's focus on this purpose for writing.

When we asked you last week for some definitions [of poetry], most of you had definitions about imagination. But poetry can also be fun. It can be humorous. And those people who come from Kerry's homeland, Ireland...[pause] the Irish have developed a form of a poem called a limerick.

You must try and have the last line to be a little bit of a surprise—to sort of complete the thoughts that happen up here, but a little bit of a surprise. And it should have a bit of humor. So, they are called...[writes "limericks" on the board].

As the teacher and students worked together to create several limericks, it was apparent that one major purpose of the activity was to have fun, as well as to learn about a new form of communication. One of the most memorable exchanges I captured on tape occurred toward the end of a class in December:

Matthew: Do you know when you said you would make me start to enjoy poetry?

Norman: Yes? Am I right?

Matthew: Yes, you are.

Norman: There you go. You made my day!

I also recorded several instances of writing for the purpose of *communicating through a particular form*. For example, when a few students expressed an interest in learning to write narrative poetry, Norman indicated various purposes served by this type of poetry and explained its structure. He said that as a genre, narrative poetry tells a story, often uses rhyming couplets, and can have various themes. He then offered several examples for the students to read, including "Casey at the Bat," "Casey's Revenge," and "The Man from Snowy River." Similar dialogue was recorded during instruction in the writing of limericks, haiku, and free verse.

Finally, although I did not observe any episodes in which Norman told students their writing sessions would prepare them for future school work as they moved through the grades, he did indicate in an interview with me that he tried to be conscious that the writing activities provided in his classroom would be useful for students later. He told me that he hoped students' writing experiences in his class would make future writing assignments easier for them.

Overall, Norman emphasized to his students five major purposes for engaging in writing. Most of these purposes were communicated explicitly to the students. In his own words, Norman viewed the purpose of his writing instruction as follows:

> I guess the ultimate thing would be—I hate to use the word—but [writing is a] metacognitive thinking tool. So when they run across something they are having trouble with, they will be able to start writing and make sense of something that's confusing to them by writing. Whether it be a school thing or a personal thing or an emotional thing, it becomes something they are aware they can use in order to help sort things out. The other thing is, of course, to be able to use it [writing] for various functions—[what I] call the school things, essays and reports and all that type of thing—and to be able to do all the everyday things of writing letters to companies and ordering things and doing all of those things which I am...continuing to be surprised that so many adults can't do. They want to write a letter to complain about...the soccer coach [laughs] and they're just not able to do it and I think that sort of functional [aspect is] part of it also. But I guess if I had to say one thing, it would be the thinking, the way of sorting out ideas.

These words indicate Norman's emphasis on writing as a tool to clarify and organize thinking. He also spoke of the communicative function of writing. However, during the course of my observations in his classroom, I saw relatively few examples of students' writing for purely transactional purposes.

In other intermediate classrooms I observed, the following three additional purposes for engaging in writing were also emphasized during instruction:

- to remember or explain;
- to share with an audience; and
- to learn the stages of the writing process.

Students in other classrooms were frequently asked to write in order to *remember or explain* what had been previously listened to or read. One activity some teachers used that reflects this purpose is writing a "plot profile." After having listened to the teacher read a particular selection, the students were asked to remember and record the sequence of events and to plot these on a graph according to their perceived level of importance. Throughout such lessons, teachers emphasized that students needed to listen to the selection in order to recall the events later. However, students were also encouraged to discuss their work with one another and therefore were not required to recall the information independently. Because all the students were listening to the same story, it seemed likely that the process would lead to very similar plot profiles across the class.

In one intermediate classroom, an interesting incident occurred toward the end of one of the writing sessions. The teacher explicitly asked his students to reflect on the reasons for engaging in an activity such as the plot profile. The students offered the following possible purposes for this activity: to improve their writing (although it was unclear whether the student meant improving handwriting or improving the ability to get ideas down on paper), to prepare for a test, to remember, and to remember quickly. The students appeared unable to think of how this activity might help them with future writing. The teacher offered another purpose for writing in his conclusion to this exchange: to organize one's thoughts so the reading selection can be explained to someone else.

In several classrooms, there was also an element of writing to *discover one's own thoughts* about the topic or subject matter. In these cases, the teachers asked students to write what they thought would happen next in the story, an alternate ending, or their thoughts and feelings about a particular character. As some of these sessions continued, however, there appeared to be a growing emphasis on writing the story to include content the teachers suggested. This occurred, particularly, as teachers attempted to answer students' questions about what to write. For instance, in some classrooms, students posed a series of questions to the teacher before beginning to write, such as, "How long should it be?" "Do we begin with 'I predict?'" and "Can the main character get hurt?"

In answering these questions, teachers often provided considerable information about what to write. This may be a natural reaction for a teacher trying to encourage students to write, but it changes the purpose of the writing session from one in which students discovered thoughts about the events of a story for themselves to one in which students sought and received from the teacher the specific content and sequence of events to write about. The students requested and were given direction for their writing, with the result being that the purpose of discovery was overshadowed.

I also recorded a number of instances in which teachers emphasized writing as a means of *sharing one's work with others*, either by reading a piece informally to friends, reading it aloud to the class, or displaying it on a bulletin board. Many teachers encouraged students to work together and talk to others about their writing. Consequently, the classrooms were often quite active with students talking and reading out loud. These strategies emphasized an external but also an immediate audience for the students.

Finally, in many classrooms, writers engaged in writing for the purpose of *practicing the steps in the writing process*. Although this may seem obvious and not worthy of mention, it does indicate that, for some teachers, teaching the writing process is as important as writing *as* a process. This occurred when teachers consistently reminded the students what stage of the writing process they were engaged in and the strategies that should accompany those stages. As discussed earlier in the emphasis section of this chapter, many classrooms display charts outlining the various stages associated with the writing process: prewriting, drafting, revising, editing, and publishing. Students were encouraged to use their drafting strategies to write ideas quickly and not spend excessive time on spelling. At the revision and editing stages, students were asked to read their drafts aloud and ask themselves three questions:

1. Will it make sense to others?
2. Does it actually say what I want it to say?
3. Should I add or change words to make it easier to understand?

Proofreading strategies included reading the draft and attending to capitalization, punctuation, and spelling.

As with emphasis, ownership, and audience, Norman proved quite unique in his approach to communicating the purposes of writing to his students, both in terms of the kinds of writing activities he planned and the ways he described the purpose of these to himself and his students. All the teachers I observed seemed to provide instruction about purpose that reflected their perceptions of students' needs and experiences. Norman was more likely to articulate the purpose of a writing activity directly to his students and planned writing activities that allowed students to discover and record their thoughts, ideas, and feelings, and focused less on communicating these to others. Figure 5 indicates the various purposes for writing I discovered in observation of intermediate classrooms. Teachers of writing may find it useful to reflect on their own practices in determining the purposes they articulate to their students.

Figure 5
Purpose

✏ to discover one's own thoughts, ideas, and feelings

✏ for personal expression

✏ for enjoyment

✏ to communicate using a particular form

✏ to prepare for future school experiences

✏ to remember and to explain

✏ to communicate to others

✏ to share with an audience

✏ to learn the stages of the writing process

Reflections

Having spent six months in a variety of classrooms, I realized that each teacher exhibits different yet successful styles for teaching writing. That is, most teachers I observed articulate and implement a "writing as process" approach to their instruction, yet their classrooms looked and felt quite different from one another.

I think this is an important observation because it may help teachers who wonder how to teach writing in ways that reflect their own beliefs, personalities, teaching styles, knowledge, and experience. As I reflect on these classrooms and on my own experience, I have come to believe that we, as teachers, may not even be aware of the daily messages we give our students about the craft and task of writing. Whether we are systematic or random in our approach, whether we encourage a quiet environment or one that allows talking, whether we teach concepts individually to children or teach them to the whole group, we are, in some manner, instructing in a way that affects both what and how students write. More important, we affect how our students come to view themselves as writers. We play a very important role in our students' developing understanding of writing.

In the following two chapters, I will describe the kinds of writing activities in which students engaged. Included in this description are samples of writing produced in Norman's classroom. I will also present the students' own reflective accounts regarding their writing and their writing instruction. Taken together, students' written products and their reflective accounts tell us about the kind of writing instruction we teachers provide. And as will be apparent, our students *are* influenced by our instructional program and instructional language.

Chapter 3

What Is Done:
The Students' Writing

In separate interviews in mid-February, Steven and Sarah recounted events in which things their teachers had said played an important role in their writing. Steven was speaking of the teacher he had had the year before, and Sarah was talking about Norman, her current teacher.

> Steven: Last year, I got a B because my handwriting was messy. I would have gotten an A 'cause all of my stuff was all right. It was all there, all right. I just forgot to label two things, and my handwriting wasn't neat.

> Sarah: ...if he [Norman] wants to look at our books, I might tear a page out and write it on a new page that looks neater.

These comments bring to mind experiences I have had with students, experiences that caused me to consider my role in teaching children to write. As a teacher, I tried to encourage my students to produce both quantity and quality in their writing, but I wonder now if I emphasized one over the other in the language I used. Both Steven and Sarah refer to the teacher as being their audience for writing, and clearly that teacher-audience had emphasized neatness in handwriting; these students' comments are indicative of their understanding that writing should be produced with attention not necessarily to what it says, but to how it looks. I suspect that this was not what their teachers had intended to stress as the only—or even the primary—purpose for writing, but their instructional language clearly conveyed this message.

To determine if what teachers say and do when they teach writing affects what their students produce, it is, of course, necessary to examine students' actual written pieces. What follows in this chapter are examples and observations of students' writing collected over the five months I spent in Norman's classroom. All the writing produced by the students in school was collected by Norman. In his classroom, students kept their writing in notebooks in their desks. I am highlighting the work of Norman's students here to indicate the caliber of writing that is associated with his particular teaching strategies and style.

Kinds of Writing

Those involved in assessing and evaluating students' writing indicate that the most important source of variability in writing performance revolves around the kind of writing students are required to produce (Wilkinson, 1983). Figure 6 presents a list of the types of writing Norman's students engaged in over the five-month period of my observations. During this time, Norman involved his students in approximately 12 to 15 writing activities. As described in the previous chapter, Norman focused on poetry. His instruction consisted of such things as asking children to listen to lyrics of contemporary songs and poetry by well-known songwriters and authors; to read a

Figure 6
Kinds of Writing in Norman's Class

- limericks
- poems written on a Valentine's Day theme
- frame, "What is poetry?"
- poems written on a weather theme
- haiku
- poems written on a Christmas theme
- written responses to songs
- poems written based on a personal experience, with loss as a theme
- frames, "What is truth? Beauty? Love? Freedom? Anger?"
- notes
- rhyming couplets
- narrative poetry
- copied poem
- miscellaneous

wide variety of poems by Shakespeare, Shelley, Frost, cummings, and Pratt, among others; and to write in a variety of forms, including free verse, rhyming couplets, haiku, limericks, and narrative poems. Norman suggested topics, subjects, genres, or titles as cues to help students get started; he encouraged the students to write extensively and keep all their work in their writing notebooks, but he did not assign specific, defined writing tasks.

Overall, students from Norman's classroom each completed an average of 23 pieces of writing during the study. In this classroom, all writing in the students' notebooks was composed entirely by the students. As mentioned, Norman provided possible titles, themes, and genres for the students to use, but they did not have to write in response to these cues. Students exercised control over the topic, number, and length of the pieces they wrote. Perhaps because Norman's assignments were open-ended in nature, there was a large range in the number of pieces produced by his students: from 9 to 38.

Information concerning numbers of pieces written by my "target" students—the students I focused on during my observations—is shown in Figure 7. Norman and I selected six students from his classroom to observe (three girls and three boys) who represented various levels of writing development. We selected particular students based on observations during writing sessions, analyses of written products, and writing conferences conducted with each student. We used purposive sampling of this type to observe whether patterns of students' understanding about writing were limited to particular developmental groups.

As shown in Figure 7, Norman's students wrote varied numbers of pieces. They often produced additional writing if the suggested topic, theme, or genre was of sufficient interest. For instance, Melissa wrote 16 limericks, Jean composed 9 poems about weather, and Sarah composed 7 pieces on the "truth, beauty, freedom, or love" theme. Limericks were the most popular pieces, accounting for 24 percent of the total writing produced by the students; conversely, some topics, titles, or genres were pursued with little enthusiasm. Only Donald's writing shows a different type of pattern. He com-

Figure 7
Number of Pieces Written by Norman's Students

	Kristen	Melissa	Steven	Sarah	Donald	Jean
Limericks	3	16	2	4	2	5
Valentine theme	–	–	1	2	–	2
What is poetry?	1	2	2	1	1	3
Weather theme	2	3	2	1	1	9
Haiku	4	4	1	3	–	3
Christmas theme	1	–	1	3	1	3
Response to song	2	3	2	1	1	2
Personal experience	1	–	–	1	1	1
What is truth? etc.	3	1	1	7	1	4
Notes	–	–	–	–	–	11
Couplets	1	–	1	–	–	–
Narrative poems	1	1	–	–	–	–
Copied poem	1	1	1	1	–	–
Misc.	–	2	1	3	1	5
Total	20	33	15	27	9	38

pleted two limericks and one piece of writing in each of the remaining categories he attempted. Donald's reflective account (discussed in greater detail in the next chapter) suggested his belief that the audience for his writing was someone other than himself. In addition, during an interview with me, he stated that he would not miss writing if he could no longer do it. Donald did not seem to be interested enough in writing to care about making his own choices in relation to it, and he viewed writing assignments more or less as tasks to be completed. Overall, however, it appears that the students in this class were encouraged to exercise control over their own writing in terms of topic choice, form, and content, and this is reflected in the broad range noted in their written products.

Examples of Writing

The following writing samples were produced by the students in Norman's class when they selected the assignment that asked them to write a poem using the title "Storm." It should be noted that these writing samples were revised and edited primarily by the students themselves. However, Norman did provide assistance when conferencing individually with students in areas such as spelling, punctuation, and vocabulary. With that in mind, these writing samples are, for the most part, what the students produced as a final product.

Kristen

The rain came pelting down upon,
The ground lighted by the break of dawn,
The puddles exploded as each rain drop hit,
And the lightning flashed, the sky was lit.
Beneath a tree a boy sat down,
Sheltering himself from the rainy town,
His eyes of shame were sad and wet,
Like a still still river not flowing yet.
He sat freezing on the dark green grass,
waiting for the angry storm to pass,
His memories of home that day,

Flashed back to him as he lay,
Alone,
Cold as stone.
He'd run away from the ones who cared
But nobody had stopped him, nobody had dared
To interfere with the choice he had
to stay or leave his mom and dad.
He had chosen to leave, though there wasn't any strife
He had run away from home he had run away from life.

Melissa

Raging storm,
Howling wind,
Boats tossed at sea.

With the rain pounding,
You won't see many people,
Out at sea.

Lightning,
Thunder,
This makes bedtime a scare.
We better have a large supply of hot chocolate,
Somewhere around here.

Storms of anger
Storms with thunder
Many storms pass my way.

Howling winds
I am furious
When the rain will not quit.

Steven

Thunder
Clouds
Tornado
downpour

sneak
stranger
hiding
spying
overcast
dark
angry
revenge
murder

Sarah

Storm is a beautiful horse
that is happy and gay,
Running free on the field
My mouth sealed
Gray, gray as a storm
Not as light as a polished stone
My feeling expressed on my face
Watching Storm at a steady pace.
Suddenly my smile fades watching
Watching Storm run away
She'll be back another day!
When the day finally comes
I watch as she runs
Then she comes close I feed her buns.

Jean

Storm
Storm is wind,
that blows in the night.
It is cold,
and a eerie sight.
It is rain,
and it is angry.
It's a river,

that comes down.
The storm is over,
It's a nice sound.
It is dark,
the sun is coming down.
It is coming down,
now it's done.
We can go play,
is the springs sun.
And the river is flowing,
with the flowers just blooming.
The grass is damp,
from the storm.
It is nice,
to play in.
It gets you dirty,
the clouds come down.
It comes and covers the sun,
the storm is coming,
coming very close.
What should we do.
Oh now it's back.

Storm is cold,
a winters cold.
A mean sound,
an angry sound.
It's icy cold,
it starts to rain.
It's gloomy,
and hard to see.
And it's very ugly,
so ugly it's got an ugly face.
it's mean it wants to crunch you up.
The farm is wet damp and cold,
it's icey slippery freezing the river.

Snow
Snow, snow,
icy snow.
It's here,
have no fear.
It's cold,
but not for me,
the river is frozen.
Ready to go ice skating,
The bears are in there cave.
With the birds down in the South.

Donald

Donald did not complete a poem with the title "Storm," although he did produce the following piece in which he uses storm as a metaphor for the act of writing:

> Writing is like weather in many ways like in a story or poem. When the weather is rain. I may be crying or if it's cloudy my mind may be blury. In a storm my emotions would flare. If the wind came my thoughts would be blown past me. The sun could be bright happiness or hot anger. Light and fluffy snow would fall and it would make me happy or cheerfull. If hail fell it would be like a thumping headache.

The diverse ways students proceeded with the "Storm" writing task are noteworthy. Kristen's poem told a story, Melissa used descriptive language to indicate her feelings about the topic, Steven listed related vocabulary, and Sarah used "Storm" as the name of a horse. Jean wrote two related poems describing a storm and its aftermath. Finally, Donald described his writing of poetry as stormy in an emotional sense. These written products indicate the students' understanding that writing can be individualistic and expressive. Because they were encouraged to use the writing task to discover their own methods of working, these students came to have an evident understanding that writing can be a personally rewarding activity.

Allowing students this amount of control over their writing assignments can result in wonderfully creative written products, but it can also be a difficult step for teachers to take. Because it means that children will not produce similar pieces either in terms of quality or quantity, teachers can be put in the uncomfortable position of struggling to cover the prescribed curriculum and increasing the amount of time they need to evaluate students' writing performance. It also means that teachers' roles become more complex and less clearly defined while they try to balance intervention with prompting and responding. While it is obvious *when* Norman, for example, is engaged in one or the other of these instructional behaviors, it is less obvious *what* tells him to choose what to do. The fact that there is no authority that can tell teachers, step-by-step, how to teach writing is frustrating, but we do have access to students' written products to serve as the light that signals what needs to be taught and how.

Chapter 4

What Is Understood:
The Students' Perceptions

For me, the most worthwhile part of my venture into Norman's classroom and the other classrooms I observed was talking with children about their perceptions of writing—what enhances it, what inhibits it, and how their teachers' instructional strategies and language influence their thinking about it.

As teachers, we often make assumptions concerning the degree to which children share with us a common understanding of writing. Such assumptions are usually formed when we read our students' written products, yet completed pieces alone are an inadequate indicator of students' overall conception of writing. Because our assumptions have consequences for our instructional planning and for our expectations of students' writing performance, it is important to allow students other opportunities to reveal to us what they really think about writing. When they have opportunities to articulate their own views, we may be given the chance look into the hearts and minds of young writers and glimpse their journeys. For example, Melissa and Kristen made these comments in an interview with me.

> Robin: What happens when a writing assignment doesn't seem to fit well with you?
>
> Kristen: Well, I just can't write.
>
> Melissa: Me, too. I can just write a few sentences. If I do write a lot, it's usually not good.
>
> Kristen: I usually write a sentence, and then I have to erase and write. I just keep erasing the same sentence again. I just can't write it.
>
> Robin: And then what do you do? Do you leave it?
>
> Kristen: No. I keep working at it until the session is over. And I just never get back to it.

Clearly Kristen's and Melissa's comments would give their teacher a clearer picture of why some of their written pieces were perhaps not as strong as others, details he would not have had access to if his only source of information had been the written pieces themselves.

Investigating student perceptions as the primary medium that connects teaching and learning is the focus of this chapter. By examining students' perceptions about writing, I hope to reveal a range of information related to writing instruction. To explore these perceptions, I conducted interviews with target students from Norman's class and asked them to complete "reflective accounts," written and oral responses to open-ended questions I provided for them, as mentioned in the introduction. As I gathered students' written and oral responses in interviews or reflexive accounts, I found it useful to talk with students and question them about their perceptions while they were engaged in a writing task. Usually their comments were tape-recorded by me and later transcribed, but sometimes I used notetaking as a means of documenting their discourse. There were, however, opportunities (with Norman's help) to have students take time to write out a response to a particular query. Examples of the sorts of questions I asked appear in the appendix. In response to these questions, the students spoke candidly with me about their thoughts on (1) what good writers do, (2) the goals and purposes of writing, (3) the principal audience for writing, (4) themselves as writers, and (5) the value of writing.

What Good Writers Do

The students in Norman's class focused on what they saw as the good writer's ability to persevere, work hard, and practice. This was evident in all the reflective accounts from the target students, which are summarized in Figure 8 on the next page. Kristen, Melissa, Sarah, and Jean noted that good writers also do a lot of writing; for Jean, this meant writing long pieces, but for the others, it meant being engaged in writing for long periods of time, as often occurred in Norman's classroom. This view of what good writers do suggests an understanding that writing is not a mysterious process of inspiration alone but is accomplished with time and effort. Their teacher's emphasis on writing as craft mirrors this understanding.

Beyond the similarity in this area, however, the target students in Norman's class had differing thoughts on what good writers do. For instance, Steven, Sarah, and Jean identified being neat as a criterion for being a good writer. Interestingly, neither Kristen nor Melissa, both of whom had been identified as showing advanced writing abilities, commented on this aspect of writing. One student, Donald, noted that a good writer uses humor. In addition, students mentioned that good writers are familiar with the subjects they write about, read a lot, know the meanings of words, listen to directions, and write in an interesting way.

Norman's students' perceptions of what good writers do only partly matched the words Norman used to describe good writing and good writing habits. While Norman's instructional language emphasized the importance of perseverance, practice, neatness, and humor—all of which were mentioned by his students—he also re-

Figure 8
What Does a Good Writer Do?

Kristen	• puts a lot of effort into it
	• practices
	• works hard
Melissa	• does a lot of writing
	• shows effort, perseveres
	• concentrates
Steven	• practices
	• perseveres
	• is neat
	• writes in an interesting way
Sarah	• does a lot of writing
	• reads a lot
	• listens to directions
	• is a good handwriter
	• knows about the subject
Donald	• uses humor
	• perseveres
Jean	• practices
	• works hard
	• has neat handwriting
	• knows meanings of words
	• writes long pieces

ferred to strategies such as webbing that his students did not mention. In addition, some students offered characteristics of good writers that Norman had not talked about, such as "writes long pieces" and "listens to directions."

In Norman's class, I found the students' reflections indicated awareness of selected aspects of their teacher's instructional language, with no patterns in the nature of this awareness observed across ability levels. One exception, as mentioned, is that neither of the two students identified as advanced in writing ability (Kristen and Melissa) mentioned neatness as a criterion of good writing. Aside from this, the students' accounts reflected varied understanding of their teacher's language concerning good writing.

This mismatch between the teacher's language and the students' evident understanding may be a result of the fact that these students were in grades five and six and had already had many experiences with writing both in and out of school. Their accounts may therefore display a cumulative understanding of what good writers do. It is also possible that Norman's instructional language was not able to address the complex nature of what good writers do. As teachers, we need to be aware that our own instructional messages are continually being interpreted by our students, who attempt to fit the "new" messages into what they have heard before and what they already know.

To analyze further the relationship between these students' evident understanding of what a good writer does and their teacher's instructional language on this subject, I posed a second, related, but somewhat more explicit question: What does your teacher say you need to do to be a good writer? The most striking observation I noted in response to this question was the degree of individuality in Norman's students' comments. The students in Norman's class mentioned a variety of ways in which their teacher helped them to be better writers, with comments ranging from "He shared an analogy with me" to "He jokes and makes you feel easier." Early in February, Kristen used this example to explain Norman's approach:

> He told me when I didn't like a poem I wrote, he said, he used the analogy, he said that there's a valley and there's two mountains and you could be on this mountain but to get to the other mountain, you have to go down a bit. But you're still closer than you were there. Because I didn't like my poetry, and he said sometimes you have to go down a bit but you're still closer.

Each student reflected on something different that Norman had done or had said to them personally (student comments are summarized in Figure 9 on page 69). This seems to match the teacher's routine of instructing students through writing conferences and addressing their needs on an individual basis. For instance, Melissa commented that her teacher "helped open my imagination," while Steven said, "He showed me the difference between using ocean water, fresh water, or sparkling water in my writing." Donald noted that his teacher told him to write something "not so good" but to keep writing, a strategy that is often suggested in writing instruction manuals. Steven echoed Donald with his comment that "it doesn't have to be perfect the first time." Donald was the only student who said that his teacher helped him with spelling, punctuation, and capitalization. In addition, he commented that according to his teacher, a good writer uses a "word chain" to help develop ideas. In Norman's classroom, students were taught to create a chain of words that are somehow related as a way to develop ideas for their writing. For example, if Norman asked his students to write on the topic "blue," students provided vocabulary such as "sky, Blue Jays, unhappy, beautiful, and navy" before beginning to compose. Often the students who appeared to be stuck in their writing used this technique, creating the following type of configuration:

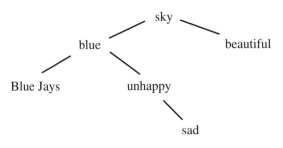

It is important to note that most of Norman's students' comments indicated instruction that emphasizes the writer rather than the writing—that is, the comments are unique and varied, suggesting the students recall Norman's advice in personal terms. Their reflections on this question do match Norman's instructional language more closely than did their comments on the question concerning the habits and techniques of good writers in general. In his instructional language, Norman did stress a personal approach to improving writing, and he was responsive to individual students' needs.

Figure 9
What Does Your Teacher Do or Say to Help You Be a Better Writer?

Kristen	• "think about writing using an analogy" • gives individual help
Melissa	• "keep writing when stuck" • "develop at own pace" • gives individual help • helps open my imagination
Steven	• "change things to make it better" • "move sentences" • "it doesn't have to be perfect the first time" • "there's a difference if you use different vocabulary"
Sarah	• "add and move lines" • gives me ideas when stuck
Donald	• "use word chain" • "write something not so good" • "practice spelling, commas, capitals"
Jean	• "write neater" • "practice" • he explains things • he jokes and it makes you feel easier

Goals and Purposes

The reflective accounts offered by the target students in Norman's class indicated an understanding that the purpose of writing goes beyond completing an assigned task; these students' reflective accounts regarding the goals and purposes of writing are summarized in Figure 10 on the next page. When I asked Norman's students questions about this subject, they responded as if they were deeply and personally involved in their writing. For the most part, their accounts indicated that writing is functional—that is, it allowed them to grow as writers but also to discover their own thoughts, ideas, and feelings. For Kristen, writing brought enjoyment, and for Melissa, Steven, and

Figure 10
Goals and Purposes of Writing

Kristen	• for enjoyment • to improve skills in writing
Melissa	• for personal expression • to aid thinking
Steven	• to describe what's in my mind • to check spelling
Sarah	• to work out problems
Donald	• to collect thoughts and put them down on paper • to write emotions • to be humorous, creative
Jean	• to practice for grades seven, eight, and nine

Sarah, writing helped with the thinking process and made explicit their tacit thoughts and ideas. Donald noted that writing helped him express emotions and be humorous and creative. Jean observed that writing in Norman's class helped her prepare for future school-related writing experiences. For each student, writing also performed a communicative function by helping them discover thoughts and ideas and then showing these to the teacher.

Norman's instructional language emphasized writing as a process of discovery, whereby students could develop a new understanding of a topic, form, or question. There does appear to be a match between Norman's instructional emphasis and his students' evident understanding of writing to discover thoughts, feelings, and ideas. Steven revealed this match quite clearly in comments he made during an interview with me in December.

> Robin: Can you tell me one thing that you think your teacher does to help you write?
>
> Steven: When he puts words up on the board and tells us just to do anything with it. Like he did before, and before

we finished talking, you knew what you were going to write. And this is kind of like a mystery. You don't know what you're going to write.

Robin: Do you like that?

Steven: Yeah, it's neat.

From my own experience, I would have to say that many students often seem uncertain when asked to reflect on the purpose for a writing task. Their typical first response when I ask them questions on this topic is "I don't know." Even when I used deeper probes such as "Are you learning something by doing this activity?" or "Is this helping you in some way?" students provide responses that do not indicate a personal involvement in their writing. Instead, I have found their responses show an understanding of writing as task oriented. This is undoubtedly related to my own instructional language and the activities I have planned for students in the past. Further, while I believe it is important and necessary for students to understand that writing is a tool they can use to organize their thoughts and to communicate, I seldom took the opportunity to inform students directly about these purposes when I was teaching. Because of this, I think it is unlikely that my students would have been able to articulate a well-considered understanding of the reasons they engaged in writing except to complete a task as requested by me, their teacher. After observing in Norman's classroom, it became apparent to me that teachers need to keep in mind that they should make explicit their goals and purposes for writing instruction to help their students develop a personal understanding about what it means to write.

Audience

When asked about the audience for their writing, the students in Norman's class showed an interesting pattern (see Figure 11). Kristen, Melissa, and Steven listed themselves as their own most important audience. Audience awareness in writing typically means being sensitive to the expectations, demands, and background of those reading the composition, yet these three students considered they

Figure 11
Audience in Writing

Kristen	• self
	• friends
	• parents
	• teacher
Melissa	• self
	• teacher
Steven	• self
	• teacher
Sarah	• parents
	• teacher
	• friends
	• self
Donald	• friend
	• teacher
Jean	• family

must please themselves first as critical readers of their writing. Several students also mentioned friends and family as important audiences for writing. Finally, information presented in Figure 11 together with Sarah's comments from the beginning of Chapter 3 indicate that Norman was also an influential audience for his students' writing. It must be noted, however, that Sarah was commenting on the teacher-audience as one that was looking for neatness in handwriting.

Overall, the target students' reflective accounts indicate only a partial match between their understanding of audience and Norman's instructional language on this subject. While Norman appeared to emphasize the self as "the writer's first reader" (Murray, 1980, p. 164), only three students' accounts suggested a match between his message and their understanding. It is instructive to note that this understanding was not demonstrated by all the students. Perhaps some students have not had the necessary experience or reached a level in their development to examine their own work critically. It is also possible that these students view writing as a transaction intended to communicate and therefore requiring an external audience. In addition, Sarah's comments from Chapter 3 raise the possibility of a mismatch between the teacher's emphasis on self as audience and the students' understanding that the teacher is the important audience in matters of neatness and handwriting.

In classrooms where teachers' instructional language emphasizes writing for an external audience, it seems logical to assume that students would not indicate an understanding that they themselves are an audience in their own writing.

Understanding Themselves as Writers

One aspect of how students view themselves as writers concerns their attitude toward writing and whether they choose to write on their own. All six target students in Norman's class reported they liked writing, although half said they did not write outside school at all (see Figure 12 on the next page). There is no clear pattern with this small group of students that an aversion to writing outside school was characteristic of a particular writing ability level. Indeed students from a variety of ability levels reported not writing outside school.

This group of students clearly articulated a positive attitude towards writing. Melissa reported liking writing, and the following conversation from early February indicates she viewed herself as a writer.

> Robin: Can you tell me a little bit about why that's your favorite poem?
>
> Melissa: I don't know. It's just I like writing narrative poems, long poems, and I like unicorns.
>
> Robin: Writing a narrative poem was your idea, wasn't it?
>
> Melissa: Yes.

Figure 12
Understanding Themselves as Writers

	Do you like to write?	Do you write outside school?
Kristen	yes	no
Melissa	yes	yes
Steven	yes	no
Sarah	yes	yes
Donald	yes	no
Jean	yes	yes

Note: Parent questionnaires verified the students' responses concerning whether they wrote outside school.

Robin:	Did you know you wanted to write that type of poem?
Melissa:	No. I just said if he [Norman] had any idea of what kind of poem, like a different poem.
Robin:	So the two of you talked together.
Melissa:	Yeah. He gave me a book with a whole bunch of famous narrative poems, and then I decided to write a narrative poem.

Such comments contradict previous research that suggests that as students get older and more through school, they seem to like writing less. This finding may indicate that it is the individual teacher rather than the students' age that influences how attitudes toward writing develop and are manifested. In all cases, the parents verified their own child's responses in this area when they responded to the questionnaire I sent home with their child.

The Value of Writing

Finding out if and how students value the writing they do was quite a challenge. I asked the students in Norman's class to respond to the following question: If you woke up tomorrow morning and found that you could no longer write, would it matter to you? All but one student (Donald) commented on what they would miss if writing were not a part of their lives.

As noted in Figure 13, the target students provided three or more examples of how they value writing. In addition to the obvious value that writing has in aiding communication, these students indicated writing was personally satisfying because it (1) allowed for personal and emotional expression; (2) made conscious one's thoughts; (3) provided enjoyment; (4) expressed humor; and (5) helped prepare for work in later grades. Their accounts again suggested a deep and personal involvement in writing. If she found she could no longer write, Kristen said, "It would take away the enjoyment of doing it," and Melissa noted, "I find it easier to express [my]self through writing something down on paper than it is to talk about your feelings."

Four of the six students reflected on the value of writing in expressing emotions or feelings. In mid-February, Sarah commented on what she would miss if writing were not a part of her life: "Then I couldn't write poems, the way I feel, and in my diary, and I write stories, and it would just be empty.... You might save trees but it would matter to me very much." Donald also mentioned this aspect of writing, although his conclusion about whether he would miss the activity was somewhat different, as is clear from the following exchange.

Robin:	Just imagine that if tomorrow you woke up in the morning and you couldn't write anymore. You could do everything else, but you couldn't write. Would it matter to you?
Donald:	[thinking] Hmm.... Does it count as numbers, too?
Robin:	Umm, no. You can still do numbers.
Donald:	Okay, all right. Not that I can think of.
Robin:	So it probably wouldn't matter too much. You could do all the other things you wanted to do?
Donald:	So far as I could think of.

There appears to be a match between Norman's emphasis on ways to help the students control their writing and students' evident

Figure 13
The Value of Writing

Kristen	• for enjoyment • to fill a need • to express feelings • to help when nervous
Melissa	• to express feelings • to help more things come to mind • to aid thinking
Steven	• to help when older • to describe what's in my mind • to help if you want to become a writer
Sarah	• for personal expression • for enjoyment • to work out feelings
Donald	• to help in future grades • to express emotions • to express humor • numbers are more valuable than writing
Jean	• something I'm used to • to communicate • to help in future grades

understanding of writing as personally valuable. In a similar vein, a match was evident between Norman's language regarding the purpose of writing as discovery oriented and his students' accounts of the value of writing to discover and express feelings, thoughts, ideas, and humor. There were, however, some notable differences among these students' accounts. Three students (Steven, Donald, and Jean) commented that writing was valuable for its potential later use, either in school or for a career. While this could indicate that these students didn't see writing as valuable in their present lives, each of them offered other responses to suggest that it is. Kristen and Melissa articulated specific functions of writing, noting that it expresses feelings, helps them when they are nervous, helps more things come to mind, and aids thinking. Jean indicated writing is an activity she is used to and one that allows for communication—particularly letter writing, which she does often. Jean said, "I'm so used to this now. And I do a lot of it at my house, so I get pretty used to doing it at school." The difference between the reflective accounts concerning value of writing may be attributable in part to ability level in writing.

Summary

In this chapter, I have detailed aspects of students' reflective accounts about writing and the relationships between these and the teacher's instructional language. In the following discussion, I will briefly summarize these relationships in an attempt to indicate what we might do in our own instructional practices to ensure that students receive the messages about writing that we hope to convey.

What good writers do. I asked students from Norman's class to think of someone who they considered to be a good writer and then talk about what he or she did to be successful in writing. The students reflected on the ability of a good writer to persevere, put forth effort, and engage in writing over extended periods. Apart from this common theme, the students provided individual responses about the nature of what good writers do. Their evident understanding suggests to me that students do not define a good writer as knowledgeable about the hands-on processes of writing, but rather as someone focused on his or her own writing. It is clear that a match exists between Norman's instructional language emphasizing writing as expressive and his students' reflective accounts about writing as a personal, individual activity. It must be noted, however, that the students in this class articulated an understanding of what a good writer does that went beyond their teacher's instructional language.

Goals and purposes of writing. Overall, the students in Norman's class considered the purpose of writing to be discovering and articulating thoughts, ideas, and feelings. Their reflective accounts match Norman's instructional language, which highlighted writing for personal expression. Only Jean indicated the purpose for writing as preparing one for future school experiences. This may be viewed as a match because Norman also articulated concern that his students be able to meet writing challenges in school.

Audience. In Norman's class, three students indicated they considered themselves to be the primary critical readers of their own writing; three students did not appear to have this sense of an internal audience. In addition, Sarah indicated that the teacher was her audience in terms of handwriting and neatness. Only a partial match seems to exist here between Norman's instructional language and students' understanding.

Students' view of themselves as writers. Norman's target students all reported that they enjoyed writing, and three out of six indicated they wrote outside of school. Norman's language emphasized that students should become personally involved in their writing and maintain control over their work, and this emphasis mirrors students' views on themselves as writers.

The value of writing. In reflecting on the value of writing in their lives, the students in Norman's class overwhelmingly offered personal reasons for engaging in the process. A match exists between Norman's language here and his students' evident understanding. However, Donald concluded that he would not miss writing if he could still do numbers, and Jean observed she would miss writing as an activity she is used to but not because it played a particular role in her life. This indicates a mismatch between Norman's language and these two students' understanding.

In reviewing what they say about writing, it is apparent that there are relationships between students' evident understanding of writing and their teacher's instructional language. This is consistent with previous research on student perceptions of teachers and instructional processes (Fear, Anderson, Englert, & Raphael, 1987; Harlin & Lipa, 1991; Kumaravadivau, 1991; Wittrock, 1986). Inconsistent findings exist as to the specific nature of these relationships (Collins, 1982).

While there was not complete agreement between what the teacher said and what the students understood about writing, these students, for the most part, understood their teacher's instructional language and were influenced by it. This is important for those of us who wonder about the effect our instruction has on our students. It is a given that students bring vast resources to their writing (King, 1980), but it is also true that individual teachers make a difference in writing instruction and that their language does influence student understanding. Teachers should therefore keep in mind that they need to follow some general practices in teaching writing. First, they need to make explicit their goals for writing instruction so that students can articulate a sense of what they are learning. Second, teachers should strive to help students develop an awareness of both an internal and an external audience for their writing. Finally, it is evident that students need opportunities to talk openly regarding their perceptions about writing and about themselves as writers. This is important so that teachers can change or continue their own instructional practices based on what their students tell them.

Chapter 5

Thoughts on How to Teach Writing

Learning to write has been likened to weaving a "delicate tapestry" (Smith, 1982). The vignettes from the intermediate classroom presented in this book show that students learn to weave their own individual tapestries even if they have been exposed to the same instructional strategies and approaches. What they produce depends on many factors, including the important one of how they make sense of their task—that is, what meaning they ascribe to the writing instruction their teachers deliver. In other words, the same instructional event can look different depending on the perceptions and interpretations of those involved.

In this final chapter I extract and synthesize from my observations and the descriptive information I gathered in Norman's classroom, other classrooms, and from my own teaching experience in order to discuss what is appropriate for writing instruction at the intermediate level. Many books give advice to aspiring writers on topics ranging from what to do about writer's block to finding ideas for book topics. Some of these books are presented in lesson format or provide exercises; in general, they are written by writers for would-be writers but are not intended specifically for use in schools. In the field of education, however, we do have access to a similar set of literature. Teachers and researchers have described their own or others' classroom practices and routines that seem particularly helpful to students and their writing. Graves (1983), Atwell (1987), and Calkins (1986) are probably the most well-known and widely read books of this kind. This book is somewhat different in that the classroom ideas and suggestions offered here come from the students themselves. The intermediate students I observed have provided us with a glimpse into their own personal understandings of writing and its instruction and have thereby offered us a means to better understand what it is we do as teachers.

In the remainder of this chapter I look at the implications these students' thoughts on their writing could have for teaching practice. I have organized these comments according to the topics used in the preceding chapter, topics that emerged as important for writing during the course of my classroom observations and interviews. Figure 14 outlines these topics in web form.

What Good Writers Do

It is important for teachers to focus on students' prior knowledge of strategies for good writing in order to expand on that knowledge and correct misunderstandings that may have developed over time. For instance, Susan had this to say about what she thought made one of her peers a good writer: "I think she likes to read and her writing is nice—it's not sloppy. It's not terrific; it's just neat and nice." This student clearly believed that neat handwriting was an extremely important part of good writing. This is necessary information for the teacher to have because, without further instruction

Figure 14
Important Areas for Writing Instruction

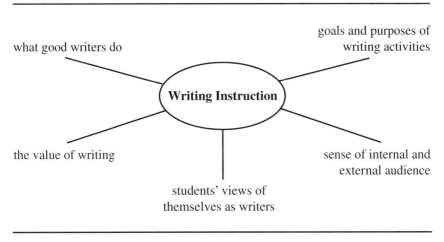

and clarification, Susan will have little chance of improving her own writing. On the other hand, the following comments were made by students who seemed to have a strong sense of what is important for good writing:

- ☞ "They put a lot of effort into it and stay with it until it's done."
- ☞ "I guess they put a lot of effort into it, and they practice at it. They write a lot of different kinds, too."
- ☞ "I think they have to work at it."
- ☞ "If you've read a book about, say, whales, and then you have to write a piece on whales, it comes easy because you know information and you can think up a story."

Such comments should indicate to teachers that these students already know a great deal about specific behaviors associated with good writing. The teachers' job now is to help students draw on this knowledge during writing. To do this, teachers need to provide students with opportunities to express themselves and must listen to what their students have to say. Open-ended questions and informal discussions can allow students to transform what may be hazy thoughts about writing into concrete and tangible ideas. Instructional scaffolding can also help students identify what they know about good writing and expand on that knowledge. The steps involved are as follows:

1. An adult listens to the student read his or her own text.
2. The adult asks questions about the meaning and content of the text.
3. The adult then expands on the meaning of the text.

With practice, these instructional techniques will provide students with greater control over their own thought processes.

This, of course, has implications for assessment and evaluation. For instance, recall and standardized tests may provide useful information about group performance, but they are less helpful for planning instruction for individual students. Teachers have an important role to play in identifying student needs, which can then be addressed most effectively through individual instruction. To improve instruction in this way, teachers must be encouraged to rely on their own observations as a form of assessment and be given the opportunity and support to assess individual students on an individual basis. We know there are many ways to learn; now we must find ways to assess and instruct students that acknowledge their individual learning styles.

As teachers get to know their students during the school year, they become better able to assess how individual children learn and how best to assist in their learning processes. As Marshall (1989) observed, *assess* has its roots in the Latin *assidére*, which means "to sit beside." This sort of assessment is something I observed over and over in Norman's classroom as he sat with individual students to gain insight into how they were writing and why. What this suggests to me is that as teachers of writing, our focus needs to be less on what to teach when and more on how children learn and how to support that learning. This focus requires observations of individual children rather than just attention to their writing.

In addition to observation, it may be desirable to use other forms of assessment to gain a comprehensive view of individual students' understanding of writing and its instruction. These forms might include recorded observations, student surveys, parent surveys, individual and small-group conferences, student self-evaluations, portfolios, and case studies. Assessment methods such as these can provide opportunities for teachers to access students' broad understanding of the instruction they receive. As this book indicates, this may be particularly appropriate in the intermediate grades, when students are developing increased abilities to express their ideas and thoughts on such subjects.

Goals and Purposes

One of the most telling incidents that occurred in a classroom in which I observed followed an activity in which the students plotted the events of a story on a graph. This teacher very courageously asked his students in my presence to comment on their perceptions of the purpose of the activity in which they had been involved. Much to the teacher's disappointment, the students seemed either not to know the purpose of the activity or said that it was intended to help them prepare for later tests, improve handwriting, or increase writing speed.

Gundlach (1982) argues that teachers and researchers used to assume that children were unable to understand the purposes for writing and writing activities in school. This assumption has led to instruction that teaches writing as a code that involves spelling, punctuation, and organization but does not emphasize creativity or personal expression. It appears from the students' reflective accounts in this study, however, that when a teacher does focus attention on the purposes of writing and explains these directly to students, they are able to understand and internalize these purposes. It may well be valuable for teachers to talk with intermediate-level students about the purposes of the writing tasks they are assigned. Such instruction would be in keeping with Halliday's (1975) ideas of "intentionality" in language learning. According to Applebee and

Langer (1984), intentionality exists when "the task has a clear over-all purpose driving any separate activity that may contribute to the whole. Eventual evaluation of students' success can be cast in terms of what they intended to accomplish" (p. 185).

Teachers who are able to access and develop students' intentionality are in a better position to assess each student's progress. Writing workshops, with their emphasis on conferences, offer an opportunity for students to reveal their perceptions of purpose and for teachers to clarify any misunderstandings. In conferences, teachers need to ask a questions such as "What do you think you are learning by doing this activity?" followed by probing questions such as "Can you tell me more?" Teachers can make explicit their own reasons for assigning certain writing tasks, but students should be allowed to develop their own goals and purposes for writing. As in other areas of writing instruction, teachers and students need to work together to establish a balance between teacher- and student-determined goals and approaches.

Audience

From the earliest years, students are called on to write in school. By the time they reach the intermediate grades, it seems obvious to many that writing is something one does for the teacher. But many researchers and teachers argue that students need to develop an understanding that writing is done sometimes for an external audience and sometimes for oneself. This acknowledges the dual nature of writing: to make personal meaning and to communicate that meaning. Howard and Barton (1988) state that an overemphasis on writing to communicate "overlooks writing's first meaning-making or articulation phase, which is so crucial to getting started" (p. 25).

As teachers, we need to ask students about audience awareness to gauge the influence of our teaching and of previous instruction. Short inventories or monthly conferences would provide opportunities to gather systematic information of this sort. Instruction could then take the form of writing activities that allow students to engage in both expressive writing, during which they can discover their own thoughts, ideas, and feelings, and transactional writing, in which they transmit information or ideas. It is important to acknowledge this dual nature of writing when teaching, particularly in light of observations made by Applebee (1982) and others who discuss the less than ideal character of instruction that asks students essentially to transcribe information found in previously written texts and assumes "an audience whose body of relevant information is both larger and better articulated than the writer's own" (p. 378). Applebee's statement suggests that students should be encouraged both to write on self-selected topics that may be unfamiliar to the teacher and to engage in expressive writing. Graves (1991) and Atwell (1987) also recommend that teachers reduce their reliance on prepared materials such as story starters and encourage students to develop their own topics for writing. In addition, Graves suggests that students write to real audiences—friends, parents, a newspaper, a favorite book author, and so on—who might respond to the messages.

Of course, students who are involved primarily in transactional writing do so for an external audience. While it is important for students to consider audience when writing, instruction needs to emphasize a balance between the needs of the writer and the needs of a reader. Younger students particularly may require specific instruction in the area of developing a sense of inner audience because many of them will have experienced writing only as something to be commented on by the teacher or a parent. To that end, teachers need to incorporate self-assessment into the writing process so that students can learn to evaluate writing they have written for themselves for their own reasons. This type of writing remains important through the years and therefore should be emphasized by teachers at all levels. As Andrasick (1990) points out, expressive writing even at the high school level "releases students from the fear of being wrong and allows them to acknowledge their personal responses" (p. 42).

Teachers I have observed displayed individual strengths when it came to instruction in the area of audience. Some highlighted the importance of inner audience, while others spent time and energy instructing their students about external audience. What is needed is a balance between the two. Our students need to choose topics for themselves and write about them with sensitivity to their audience, whether internal or external.

Students' Views of Themselves as Writers

The majority of the students I spoke with reported that they enjoyed writing, but fewer indicated they engaged in writing outside of school. One noteworthy pattern is that *all* the older students—that is, those in Norman's class—said they enjoyed writing. King (1980) and other researchers have suggested that as students get older, they report decreasing enjoyment of writing, but clearly this trend was not observed in my study. Although it must be acknowledged that I relied on self-reports that may have been influenced by the participants' desire to please me or help me in some way, the data suggest that Norman's emphasis on individual instruction, self as audience, and expressive writing were influential in affecting his students' positive views of themselves as writers. In this case, it seems that Norman's influence and the freedom he gave students to respond in their own ways to writing assignments were the important factors. This finding is supported by Hudson (1986), who stated, "As children gain more control in the amount, content, and format of writing, they are more likely to perceive it as their own even if a teacher has made the assignment" (p. 65).

The very nature of expressive writing offers the writer opportunities to make personal responses and thereby take ownership of his or her work. These responses should then be validated by the teacher. Judging by Norman's students' positive attitudes about writing and themselves as writers, it seems that rather than decreasing the amount of expressive writing assigned as students get older, some expressive writing should be continued throughout the grades.

The Value of Writing

In this study, Norman emphasized the value of writing to express thoughts, ideas, and feelings, and his students appeared to see writing as something of personal value in their lives. On the other hand, when other teachers I observed emphasized the value of writing to communicate to others, their students appeared to be unsure of the value of writing. In other words, students whose teachers stressed writing as a communication tool *only* did not necessarily make the leap (as we teachers hope they will) to understand that writing can be personally relevant and valuable to their lives. Norman's students, for the most part, seemed able to make this leap. This is likely due to instructional practices that were geared to the individual writer and to "think-aloud" modeling strategies. In the first instance, Norman instructed individual students using their own writing as a starting point. Students did not have to wonder how their teacher's lesson applied to their writing—they knew. In the second instance, Norman's think-aloud practices ensured that students understood it is appropriate and desirable to think about and question their writing in process. Because he modeled "getting stuck" as a writer, Norman's students did not give up when this happened to them. Instead, they persevered and learned that their writing was something they did for themselves.

Some Further Ideas

Andrasick (1990) suggests that teaching means affecting how students process information. It follows that, as teachers of writing, we need to employ procedures that reveal how that processing occurred. Think-aloud protocols, a valuable strategy for researchers, can be adapted for use in the classroom, as Norman has done, so that teachers can monitor students' thought processes on a regular basis. For example, the teacher could compose a short text on a transparency with an overhead projector or on a computer with a projected screen; while writing, he or she can talk about thoughts and goals for the piece. From there, the teacher and students can "walk through" the piece together, changing details, rearranging events, or polishing mechanics.

Finally, it would be worthwhile for teachers to invite published writers from the community to their classrooms to describe their writing processes. Writers unions and other professional organizations can often provide lists of writers who might be willing to do school visits, and some public library systems have "writer-in-residence" programs that bring writers to smaller communities. In addition, publishers or local bookstores can sometimes arrange for authors to come to certain areas as part of a promotional tour for a new publication.

Procedures such as these are valuable for students who may be ready to distance themselves from the physical act of writing in order to think critically about what they are doing and what they might do. Teachers may use such procedures to find out what their students say about writing and how it is taught, to assess needs, and to improve instruction. In addition, teachers should provide a range of writing experiences, so that students who may be predisposed to one form or another because of individual differences, past experiences, or level of ability will have opportunities to do well and learn new ways of expressing themselves.

Research has acknowledged that the understanding a child brings to the reading of a selection—his or her "schema" about the selection's topic—is as important to comprehension as are the actual words in the text (Rumelhart, 1981). Schema theory holds that the child "has a fund of knowledge through which he or she filters messages" (Hennings, 1984, p. 198). The results of my study indicate that students also hold schemata about writing and its instruction, and knowledge of these can better prepare teachers to provide effective writing instruction. For instance, those students who already understand and have internalized various goals and purposes for their writing require tasks that challenge them in different ways than do students who do not yet have a strong sense of purpose for writing. In the first case, students can be encouraged to make decisions about such things as what to put next, word choice, and character development, and can be asked to use their understanding of intended audience to monitor their writing process; in the second case, students might be assisted in coming up with their own topics for writing, perhaps through the use of journals or diaries, which may help them develop a sense of writing for a purpose of their own choosing.

It seems clear from looking into classrooms that students at the intermediate level do construct knowledge about writing and that a variety of factors influence that meaning-making process. It cannot be argued that children differ in how they process instructional language and in how they develop as writers. However, when we access our students' perceptions about our teaching, we are better able to offer instruction that makes sense to the child, or, as Calkins put it, "Teaching can be the cutting edge for learning" (1986, p. 60).

Appendix

Tools for Data Collection

Student Interview Questions (Reflective Accounts)

Students were asked to bring their writing folders or writing in progress to the interview. I began the interviews by making the following statement:

> As you know, I'm studying the kinds of writing students do in school. I'd like to find out what makes writing easy or difficult, fun or not fun, so I can help teachers teach writing to students like you. Today I'm going to ask you some questions about your own writing, and I'm going to tape what we say and then write it down later. Is that okay? I'd like to make sure you know this is not a test. There are no wrong answers. I only want to find out what you think about writing.

I then proceeded with questions on various topics, as listed on the following pages.

Attitudes toward Writing

1. It looks like you've written a number of pieces here. Can you tell me about them? What were the directions? What were you asked to do?

2. (a) Do you like to write? What's your favorite type of writing to do?

   (b) Is writing hard? What makes it hard?

   (c) Is writing easy? What makes it easy?

   (d) What do you write in your free time?

   (e) Is there anyone you share your writing with?

   (f) Do you like it if your teacher asks to read your work aloud?

Understanding of Writing

3. (a) Would you like to read me something you've written? [If the child declines, I asked if he or she would choose a sample of writing in progress to read to me.]

   (b) Are you happy with this piece? Why or why not?

   (c) What makes this piece of writing good or not good?

   (d) Where did you get the idea to write this piece?

   (e) What was the reason for doing this piece?

4. Think of someone you know who is a good writer. What does he or she do to be a good writer?

5. Do you ever do any writing at home? If so, what kinds of things do you write? Do you write differently at home than at school?

6. If something happened and you couldn't write any more, would it make any difference? What wouldn't you be able to do if you couldn't write?

Perceptions of Teacher's Expectations

7. (a) What does your teacher say you need to do to be a good writer? [If necessary, I probed deeper by asking, "Why

does your teacher tell you to do that?"] Do you read your teacher's comments? What do you do about them? Do they help you become a better writer? How?

(b) When you had a conference with the teacher [or another student] about this piece, what advice or help were you given?

8. Why do you think your teacher asked you to write this piece?

9. What are you learning about writing this year that is different or new from what you learned last year?

10. Are you a better writer this year than you were last year? How do you know?

11. What does your teacher do to help you become a better writer? Does it help when he [specific example of instructional strategy]? What does your teacher want you to do when you are stuck in your writing?

Perceptions of My Expectations

12. What do you think I've learned about writing from talking with you?

Teacher Interview Questions

The teacher was interviewed during a three-hour block of time arranged to take place away from the school setting. The teacher was given the interview questions a week prior to the actual interview in order to give some thought to his responses. The entire interview was audiotaped and transcribed for later analysis.

Background Information

1. How many years of teaching experience do you have? At which grade levels? In which subjects?

2. When did you decide to become a teacher, and why?

3. (a) In your university program, did you receive instruction in the teaching of writing? If so, please describe.

   (b) Was there anything you found particularly valuable in your studies about teaching writing? Was there anything lacking?

4. (a) If you have time and opportunity, do you engage in writing for pleasure or have you done so in the past?

   (b) Do you engage in writing that is job-related?

   (c) Do you ever share your own writing with your students?

The Writing Program

5. If you were asked to characterize your writing program for another teacher, what would you say? What would you emphasize?

6. What are your chief goals in helping children to write? What do you want your students to take away with them at the end of the year concerning their writing? Concerning the purpose and goals of their writing? Please specify.

7. (a) What kind of skills do you work on in writing?

   (b) What kinds of attitudes do you hope students will have about writing when they leave your classroom?

8. What do you do to help children find topics to write about?

9. (a) Which writing activities have proven most successful in the past? Why?

   (b) Least successful? Why?

   (c) Which have you abandoned? Why?

   (d) How do you think these writing activities have been perceived by the children? The ones abandoned and the ones least successful?

   (e) What was the role of purpose in these activities?

10. Think of a child who has impressed you as being a good writer. How would you describe him or her and his or her writing?

11. How would you set up a new writing task for your students?

12. How would you describe the school's context for writing?

Children's Perceptions of Writing

13. How did you become interested in the topic of student perceptions—that is, their attitudes, understandings, and interpretations—of writing?

14. (a) When a new class arrives in September, do you get a sense of how they feel about writing and why?

(b) Do you do anything to assess student perceptions at various times throughout the school year?

(c) Do you sense that perceptions change over the course of the year?

Parent Questionnaire

Parent questionnaires were sent home with each of the target students to provide additional information concerning the students' writing, past and present writing habits, the extent to which writing was observed at home, and reading behaviors. In addition, parents were asked to comment on their child's interests and hobbies. These data were used to substantiate classroom observation findings and students' interviews. All questionnaires were returned to Norman, the classroom teacher, within a two-week time frame.

Child's Name: _____

Birthdate: _____ Age:_____

This questionnaire will help me gain information concerning your child's perceptions of the writing process. It is concerned with your child's view of writing text and not particularly with his or her handwriting.

1. (a) At what age did your child show an interest in printing or drawing? _____

   (b) Have you kept any of these early efforts? _____

2. How much interest did your child show in printing or drawing before coming to school?

   A lot _____ Some _____ Not much _____

3. (a) How does your child feel about the writing she or he does in school? _____

   _____

   (b) Do you display the writing that comes from school? If so, how? _____

   _____

4. Do you have any concerns about your child's writing development? _____

   _____

5. (a) Does your child show any interest in writing outside of school? _____

   (b) If so, what kinds of writing does your child do outside of school? _____

   _____

6. Where does your child usually write? (kitchen table, playroom, etc.) _____

   _____

7. Do you deliberately involve your child in any writing activities at home? (shopping list, letters to grandparents, etc.) Please describe. _____

   _____

8. (a) Does your child like to draw? _____

(b) If so, what? _____

_____

9. Please describe your child's interests, hobbies, or sports activities. _____

_____

_____

10. Please describe any writing that you or other adults at your home do that your child might see you doing. _____

_____

_____

11. Do you think your child sees him- or herself as a successful writer? _____

12. (a) Does your child enjoy reading? _____

(b) Being read to? _____

(c) Where does your child get books to read? (e.g., library, purchased or given as gifts, school, older siblings, etc.)

_____

_____

Form completed by: _____

Schedule for Data Collection and Analysis

On the following page I have detailed the steps I took to collect and analyze data during my study of writing instruction in the middle grades.

Data Collection

June–August	October	November	December	January	February
• Conduct pilot study • Refine instruments	• Conduct teacher/interviews • Begin informal classroom visits • No recording of data • Send home parent questionnaire	Classroom observations for each class → Week 1: 2.0 hours Week 2: 3.0 hours Week 3: 4.0 hours Week 4: 5.0 hours	Week 1: 5.5 hours Week 2: 6.0 hours	Week 1: 7.0 hours Week 2: 8.0 hours Week 3: 9.0 hours Week 4: 9.0 hours	• Schedule any missed observation sessions • Conduct student interviews

Data Analysis

June–August	October	November	December	January	February
• Pilot methodologies for accessing students' understandings of writing	• Transcribe interview data • Set up profiles for individual children and teachers • Code/analyze parent questionnaires	• Collect and copy children's writing • Code field notes • Transcribe audio- and videotapes • Review interview data with teachers	• Collect and copy children's writing • Code field notes • Transcribe audio- and videotapes	• Collect and copy children's writing • Code field notes • Transcribe audio- and videotapes	• Transcribe student interview data • Begin formal analysis

Study will yield the following data sources:
1. 2 hours of teacher interviews
2. 12 hours of student interviews
3. 107 hours of classroom observation (58.5 hours per class)
   —field notes and transcriptions of instructional language
4. 12 parent questionnaires
5. Samples of children's writing

References

Andrasick, K. (1990). *Opening texts: Using writing to teach literature.* Portsmouth, NH: Heinemann.

Applebee, A. (1982). Writing and learning in school settings. In M. Nystrand (Ed.), *What writers know: The language, process, and structure of written discourse* (pp. 365–381). Orlando, FL: Academic.

Applebee, A. (1991). Environments for language teaching and learning: Contemporary issues and future directions. In J. Flood, J.M. Jensen, D. Lapp, & J.R. Squire (Eds.), *Handbook of research on teaching the English language arts* (pp. 549–556). New York: Macmillan.

Applebee, A., & Langer, J. (1984). Instructional scaffolding: Reading and writing as natural language activities. In J. Jensen (Ed.), *Composing and comprehending* (pp. 185–190). Urbana, IL: National Council of Teachers of English.

Atwell, N. (1987). *In the middle.* Portsmouth, NH: Heinemann.

Beach, R. (1977). *Writing about ourselves and others.* Urbana, IL: National Council of Teachers of English.

Bereiter, C., & Scardamalia, M. (1983). Levels of inquiry in writing research. In P. Mosenthal, L. Tamor, & S. Walmsley (Eds.), *Research on writing: Principles and methods* (pp. 3–25). White Plains, NY: Longman.

Berthoff, A. (1981). *The making of meaning: Metaphors, models, and maxims for writing teachers.* Portsmouth, NH: Heinemann.

Bradbury, R. (1980). *The stories of Ray Bradbury.* New York: Knopf.

Brannon, L. (1985). Toward a theory of composition. In B. McClelland & T. Donovan (Eds.), *Perspectives on research and scholarship in composition* (pp. 6–25). New York: Modern Language Association of America.

Britton, J., Burgess, T., Martin, N., McLeod, A., & Rosen, H. (1975). *Schools Council (Great Britain) project on written language of 11–18 year olds.* London: Macmillan.

Calkins, L.M. (1986). *The art of teaching writing.* Portsmouth, NH: Heinemann.

Cambourne, B. (1988). *The whole story: Natural learning and the acquisition of literacy in the classroom.* Richmond Hill, ON: Scholastic.

Clay, M.M. (1991). *Becoming literate: The construction of inner control.* Portsmouth, NH: Heinemann.

Collins, C. (1985). The power of expressive writing in reading comprehension. *Language Arts, 62*(1), 48–54.

Collins, J. (1982). Discourse style, classroom interaction and differential treatment. *Journal of Reading Behavior, 14*(4), 429–437.

Donovan, T., & McClelland, B. (1980). *Eight approaches to teaching composition.* Urbana, IL: National Council of Teachers of English.

Dyson, A.H., & Freedman, S.W. (1991). Writing. In J. Flood, J.M. Jensen, D. Lapp, & J.R. Squire (Eds.), *Handbook of research on teaching the English language arts* (pp. 754–776). New York: Macmillan.

Emig, J. (1971). *The composing processes of twelfth graders.* Urbana, IL: National Council of Teachers of English.

Fear, K.L., Anderson, L.M., Englert, C.S., & Raphael, T.E. (1987). The relationship between teachers' beliefs and instruction and students' conceptions about the writing process. In J.E. Readence & R.S. Baldwin (Eds.), *Research in literacy: Merging perspectives* (36th yearbook of the National Reading Conference, pp. 255–263). Rochester, NY: National Reading Conference.

Flower, L., & Hayes, J. (1981). Plans that guide the composing process. In C. Frederiksen & J. Dominic (Eds.), *Writing: Process, development and communication* (pp. 39–58). Hillsdale, NJ: Erlbaum.

Frederiksen, C., & Dominic, J. (Eds.). (1981). *Writing: Process, development and communication* (Vol. 1 of *Writing: The nature, development and teaching of written communication*). Hillsdale, NJ: Erlbaum.

Graves, D.H. (1975). An examination of the writing processes of seven year old children. *Research in the Teaching of English, 9,* 227–241.

Graves, D.H. (1983). *Writing: Teachers & children at work.* Portsmouth, NH: Heinemann.

Graves, D.H. (1985). *Write from the start: Tapping your child's natural writing ability.* New York: Dutton.

Graves, D.H. (1991). All children can write. In B. Power & R. Hubbard (Eds.), *Literacy in process* (pp. 67–78). Portsmouth, NH: Heinemann.

Gundlach, R. (1982). Children as writers: The beginnings of learning to write. In M. Nystrand (Ed.), *What writers know: The language, process and structure of written discourse* (pp. 129–147). Orlando, FL: Academic.

Halliday, M.A.K. (1975). *Learning how to mean: Explorations in the development of language.* London: Arnold.

Harlin, R., & Lipa, S. (1991). *Understandings of process writing: Insights from children and teachers.* Paper presented at the 36th Annual Convention of the International Reading Association, Las Vegas, NV.

Hennings, D. (1984). A writing approach to reading comprehension–schema theory in action. In J. Jensen (Ed.), *Composing and comprehending* (pp. 191–200). New York: National Conference on Research in English.

Howard, V.A., & Barton, J.H. (1988). *Thinking on paper: Refine, express and actually generate ideas by understanding the process of the mind.* New York: William Morrow.

Hudson, S. (1986). Children's perceptions of classroom writing: Ownership within a continuum of control. In B. Rafoth & D. Rubin (Eds.), *The social construction of written communication* (pp. 37–69). Norwood, NJ: Ablex.

Irwin, J.A., & Doyle, M.A. (Eds.). (1992). *Reading/writing connections: Learning from research*. Newark, DE: International Reading Association.

Juliebö, M.F., & Edwards, J. (1989, January). Encouraging meaning making in young writers. *Young Children*, 22–27.

King, M. (1980). Learning how to mean in written language. *Theory into Practice, 19*(3), 163–169.

Kumaravadivau, B. (1991). Language-learning tasks: Teacher intention and learner interpretation. *ELT Journal, 45*(2), 98–107.

Langer, J., & Applebee, A. (1987). *How writing shapes thinking: A study of teaching and learning*. Urbana, IL: National Council of Teachers of English.

Lauer, J. (1980). The rhetorical approach: Stages of writing and strategies for writers. In T. Donovan & B. McClelland (Eds.), *Eight approaches to teaching composition* (pp. 53–64). Urbana, IL: National Council of Teachers of English.

Marshall, J.D. (1989). *Patterns of discourse in classroom discussion of literature*. Report prepared for the Centre for Learning and Teaching of Literature, University at Albany, Albany, New York: U.S. Department of Education.

Moffet, J. (1981). *Active voice: A writing program across the curriculum*. Portsmouth, NH: Heinemann.

Murray, D. (1980). Writing as process: How writing finds its own meaning. In T. Donovan & B. McClelland (Eds.), *Eight approaches to teaching composition* (pp. 3–20). Urbana, IL: National Council of Teachers of English.

Murray, D. (1982). *Learning by teaching: Selected articles on writing and teaching*. Portsmouth, NH: Heinemann.

Murray, D. (1991). Getting under the lightning. In B. Power & R. Hubbard (Eds.), *Literacy in process* (pp. 5–13). Portsmouth, NH: Heinemann.

Rumelhart, D. (1981). *Understanding understanding*. (Technical Rept.). California University, San Diego, CA: Center for Human Information Processing.

Shanklin, N. (1991). Whole language and the writing process: One movement or two? *Topics in Language Disorders, 11*(3), 45–57.

Smith, F. (1982). *Writing and the writer*. New York: Holt, Rinehart.

Suhor, C. (1984). Thinking visually about writing: Three models for teaching composition, K–12. In C. Thaiss & C. Suhor (Eds.), *Speaking and writing, K–12: Classroom strategies and the new research*. Urbana, IL: National Council of Teachers of English.

Tierney, R.J., & Shanahan, T. (1991). Research on the reading-writing relationship: Interactions, transactions, and outcomes. In R. Barr, M.L. Kamil, P. Mosenthal & P.D. Pearson (Eds.), *Handbook of reading research: Volume II* (pp. 246–280). White Plains, NY: Longman.

Walmsley, S. (1983). Writing disability. In P. Mosenthal, L. Tamor, & S. Walmsley (Eds.), *Research on writing: Principles and methods* (pp. 227–286). White Plains, NY: Longman.

Wason-Ellam, L. (1987). Writing across the curriculum. *Canadian Journal of English Language Arts*, *11*(3), 5–23.

Wilkinson, A. (1983). Assessing language development: The Crediton project. In A. Freedman, I. Pringle, & J. Yalden (Eds.), *Learning to write: First language/second language*. White Plains, NY: Longman.

Wittrock, M.C. (1986). *Handbook of research on teaching*. New York: Macmillan.

Suggested Further Reading

Adelman, C. (1981). *Uttering, muttering: Collecting, using and reporting talk for social and educational research.* London: McIntyre.

Applebee, A. (1984). *Contexts for learning to write: Studies of secondary school instruction.* Norwood, NJ: Ablex.

Au, K. (1980). Participation structures in a reading lesson with Hawaiian children: Analysis of a culturally appropriate instructional event. *Anthropology and Education Quarterly, 9*(2), 91–115.

Bellack, A., Kliebard, H., Hyman, R., & Smith, F. (1966). *The language of the classroom.* New York: Teachers College Press.

Berkenkotter, C., & Murray, D. (1983). Decisions and revisions: The planning strategies of a publishing writer, and response of a laboratory rat—or, being protocoled. *College Composition and Communication, 34,* 156–172.

Bialystok, E., & Ryan, E. (1985). A metacognitive framework for the development of first and second language skills. In D. Forrest-Pressley, G. MacKinnon, & T. Waller (Eds.), *Metacognition, cognition and human performance* (Vol. 1). Orlando, FL: Academic.

Birnbaum, J., & Emig, J. (1991). Case study. In J. Flood, J.M. Jensen, D. Lapp, & J.R. Squire (Eds.), *Handbook of research on teaching the English language arts* (pp. 195–204). New York: Macmillan.

Bisanz, J., Bisanz, G., & Kail, R. (1983). *Learning in children: Progress in cognitive development research.* New York: Springer-Verlag.

Black, J., & Martin, R. (1982). Children's concepts about writing at home and school. In J. Niles & L. Harris (Eds.), *New inquiries in reading research and instruction* (pp. 300–304). New York: National Reading Conference.

Blank, M. (1975). Eliciting verbalization from young children in experimental tasks. *Child Development, 46,* 254–257.

Bloome, D. (1991). Anthropology and research on teaching the English language arts. In J. Flood, J.M. Jensen, D. Lapp, & J.R. Squire (Eds.), *Handbook of research on teaching the English language arts* (pp. 46–56). New York: Macmillan.

Bloome, D., & Bailey, F. (1992). Studying language and literacy through events, particularity, and intertextuality. In R. Beach, J.L. Green, M.L. Kamil, & T. Shanahan (Eds.), *Multidisciplinary perspectives on literacy research* (pp. 181–210). Urbana, IL: National Council of Teachers of English.

Bloome, D., & Green, J.L. (1982). The social contexts of reading: A multidisciplinary perspective. In B.A. Hutson (Ed.), *Advances in reading/language research* (Vol. 1). Greenwich, CN: JAI Press.

Bloome, D., Harris, O., & Ludlum, D. (1991). Reading and writing as sociocultural activities: Politics and pedagogy in the classroom. *Topics in Language Disorders, 11*(3), 14–27.

Bloome, D., & Nieto, S. (1990). Children's understanding of basal readers. *Theory into Practice, 23*(4), 258–264.

Bogdan, R.C., & Bicklen, S.K. (1982). *Qualitative research for education: An introduction to theory and methods.* Needham Heights, MA: Allyn & Bacon.

Bohm, D. (1980). *Wholeness and the implicate order.* London: Routledge & Kegan Paul.

Bracewell, R. (1983). Investigating the control of writing skills. In P. Mosenthal, L. Tamor, & S. Walmsley (Eds.), *Research on writing.* White Plains, NY: Longman.

Britton, J. (1982). Spectator role and the beginnings of writing. In M. Nystrand (Ed.), *What writers know: The language, process and structure of written discourse* (pp. 149–169). Orlando, FL: Academic.

Bruner, J. (1960). *The process of education.* Cambridge, MA: Harvard University Press.

Buckingham, D. (1992). Media education: The limits of a discourse. *Journal of Curriculum Studies, 24*(4), 297–313.

Cairney, T. (1988, January). The purpose of basals: What children think. *The Reading Teacher,* 420–428.

Calkins, L.M. (1985). Forming research communities among naturalistic researchers. In B. McClelland & T. Donovan (Eds.), *Perspectives on research and scholarship in composition* (pp. 125–145). New York: Modern Language Association of America.

Cazden, C. (1986). Classroom discourse. In M. Wittrock (Ed.), *Handbook of research in education.* New York: Macmillan.

Cazden, C. (1988). *Classroom discourse: The language of teaching and learning.* Portsmouth, NH: Heinemann.

Clark, C., & Florio, S. (1983). Understanding writing instruction: Issues of theory and method. In P. Mosenthal, L. Tamor & S. Walmsley (Eds.), *Research on writing: Principles and methods* (pp. 236–266). White Plains, NY: Longman.

Coe, D. (1986). *Three views of writing: Perceptions of a child, her parents and her teacher.* (ED 282 237)

Corsaro, W.A. (1981). Entering the child's world: Research strategies for field entry and data collection in a preschool setting. In J.L. Green & C. Wallat (Eds.), *Ethnography and language in educational settings* (pp. 117–146). Norwood, NJ: Ablex.

Cuban, L. (1984). *How teachers taught: Constancy and change in American classrooms, 1890–1980.* White Plains, NY: Longman.

Curtis, S. (1990). Whole language evaluation strategies: Examining the doughnut instead of the whole. In E. Daly (Ed.), *Monitoring children's language development*. Victoria, Australia: Australian Reading Association.

Daly, E. (Ed.). (1990). *Monitoring children's language development*. Victoria, Australia: Australian Reading Association.

Delamont, S. (1976). *Interaction in the classroom: Contemporary sociology of the school*. London: Methuen.

Dobbert, M. (1982). *Ethnographic research*. New York: Praeger.

Donaldson, H. (1978). *Children's minds*. New York: Norton.

Dorr-Bremme, D. (1990). Contextualization cues in the classroom: Discourse regulation and social control functions. *Language in Society, 19*, 379–402.

Driscoll, A., Peterson, K., Browning, M., & Stevens, D. (1990). Teacher evaluation in early childhood education: What information can young children provide? *Child Study Journal, 20*(2), 67–79.

Duckworth, E. (1987). *The having of wonderful ideas and other essays on teaching and learning*. New York: Teachers College Press.

Dyson, A.H. (1984). *Understanding the how's and why's of writing: The development of children's concepts of writing in primary classrooms* (Second Grade Data, Vol. 2, Research Rep.). Urbana, IL: National Council of Teachers of English.

Dyson, A.H. (1985). Writing and the social lives of children. *Language Arts, 62*(6), 632–639.

Emig, J. (1981). Non-magical thinking: Presenting writing developmentally in schools. In C. Frederiksen & J. Dominic (Eds.), *Writing: Process, development and communication* (pp. 21–30). Hillsdale, NJ: Erlbaum.

Faigley, L. (1985). *Assessing writers' knowledge and processes of composing*. Norwood, NJ: Ablex.

Farr, M. (Ed.). (1985). *Introduction of advances in writing research: Children's early writing development*. Norwood, NJ: Ablex.

Fear, K. (1990). *The relationship between teacher conceptions about writing instruction and student perceptions and performance in writing*. Unpublished dissertation, Michigan State University, East Lansing, Michigan.

Flanders, N.A. (1974). *Interaction analysis handbook*. St. Paul, MN: Paul S. Amidon.

Florio, S., & Clark, C. (1982). The functions of writing in an elementary classroom. *Research in the Teaching of English, 16*(2), 115–129.

Fraser, B. (1981). *Evaluation in education: An international review series*. New York: Pergamon.

Freedman, S. (1987). *Response to student writing*. Urbana, IL: National Council of Teachers of English.

Freeman, E., & Sanders, T. (1987, April). *Probing children's concepts of writing functions: A developmental research instrument*. Paper presented at the Annual Meeting of the American Educational Research Association, Washington, DC.

Freire, P. (1985). *The politics of education: Culture, power and liberation.* South Hadley, MA: Bergin & Garvey.

Gannaway, H. (1977). Making sense of school. In M. Stubbs & S. Delamont (Eds.), *Explorations in classroom observation.* New York: Wiley.

Geertz, C. (1973). *The interpretation of cultures.* New York: Basic.

Glaser, B., & Strauss, A. (1967). *The discovery of grounded theory: Strategies for qualitative research.* New York: de Gruyter.

Good, T., & Brophy, T. (1973). *Looking in classrooms.* New York: HarperCollins.

Goodlad, J. (1984). *A place called school: Prospects for the future.* New York: McGraw-Hill.

Gordon, C. (1990). A study of students' text structure revisions. *English Quarterly, 23*(1–2), 7–28.

Green, J.L., & Wallat, C. (1981). *Ethnography and language in educational settings.* Norwood, NJ: Ablex.

Gumperz, J.J. (1981). Conversational inference and classroom learning. In J.L. Green & C. Wallat (Eds.), *Ethnography and language in educational settings* (pp. 3–24). Norwood, NJ: Ablex.

Gundlach, R. (1981). On the nature and development of children's writing. In C. Frederiksen & J. Dominic (Eds.), *Writing: Process, development and communication* (pp. 133–152). Hillsdale, NJ: Erlbaum.

Hamilton-Wieler, S. (1990). If I missed the day you taught me how to write, I'm sorry. *English Quarterly, 23*(3–4), 11–14.

Harste, J., Burke, C., & Woodward, V. (1982). Children's language and world: Initial encounters with print. In J.A. Langer & M.T. Smith-Burke (Eds.), *Reader meets author/bridging the gap* (pp. 105–131). Newark, DE: International Reading Association.

Harste, J., Woodward, V., & Burke, C. (1984). *Language stories and literacy lessons.* Portsmouth, NH: Heinemann.

Hatch, J. (1990). Young children as informants in classroom studies. *Early Childhood Research Quarterly, 5,* 251–264.

Hayes, J., & Flower, L. (1983). Uncovering cognitive processes in writing: An introduction to protocol analysis. In P. Mosenthal, L. Tamar, & S. Walmsley (Eds.), *Research on writing: Principles and methods* (pp. 206–220). White Plains, NY: Longman.

Heath, S.B. (1983). *Ways with words: Language, life and work in communities and classrooms.* Cambridge, UK: Cambridge University Press.

Hillocks, G. (1986). *Research on written communication: New directions for teaching.* New York: National Conference on Research in English.

Hitchcock, G., & Hughes, D. (1989). *Research and the teacher: A qualitative introduction to school-based research.* New York: Routledge.

Holdaway, D. (1979). *The foundations of literacy.* Sydney, Australia: Scholastic.

Kinneavey, J. (1991). Rhetoric. In J. Flood, J.M. Jensen, D. Lapp & J.R. Squire (Eds.), *Handbook of research on teaching the English language arts* (pp. 633–642). New York: Macmillan.

Kohak, E. (1985). *The embers and the stars: A philosophical inquiry into the moral sense of nature.* Chicago, IL: University of Chicago Press.

Kress, G. (1985). *Linguistic processes in sociocultural practice.* Victoria, Australia: Deakin University Press.

Kucer, S.B. (1991). Authenticity as the basis for instruction. *Language Arts, 68*(7), 532–540.

Lauer, J., & Asher, J. (1988). *Composition research: Empirical designs.* New York: Oxford University Press.

Lemke, J. (1985). *Using language in the classroom.* Victoria, Australia: Deakin University Press.

Lindsay, J.S. (1990). Classroom discourse analysis: A review of the literature with implications for educational evaluation. *Journal of Research and Development in Education, 23*(2), 107–116.

Lopate, P. (1978). Helping young children start to write. In C. Cooper & L. Odell (Eds.), *Research on composing: Points of departure* (pp. 135–145). Urbana, IL: National Council of Teachers of English.

Lortie, D.C. (1975). *Schoolteacher.* Chicago, IL: University of Chicago Press.

Macrorie, K. (1976). *Writing to be read.* Rochelle Park, NJ: Hayden.

Mangano, N., & Allan, J. (1986). Teacher's beliefs about language arts and their effect on student beliefs and instruction. In J.A. Niles & R.V. Lalik (Eds.), *Solving problems in literacy: Learners, teachers and researchers* (pp. 135–142). Rochester, NY: National Reading Conference.

Marshall, C., & Rossman, G. (1989). *Designing qualitative research.* Newbury Park, CA: Sage.

Marshall, J.D. (1989). *Patterns of discourse in classroom discussions of literature* (Rep. of the Center for Learning and Teaching of Literature, University at Albany, State University of New York). Washington, DC: U.S. Department of Education.

Mehan, H (1979). *Learning lessons.* Cambridge, MA: Harvard University Press.

Miles, M., & Huberman, M. (1984). *Qualitative data analysis: A sourcebook of new methods.* Newbury Park, CA: Sage.

Moffet, J. (1979). Integrity in the teaching of writing. *Phi Delta Kappan, 61,* 276–279.

Morine-Dershimer, G. (1985). *Talking, listening, and learning in elementary classrooms.* White Plains, NY: Longman.

Mosenthal, P. (1983). On defining writing and classroom writing competence. In P. Mosenthal, L. Tamor, & S. Walmsley (Eds.), *Research on writing: Principles and methods* (pp. 26–74). White Plains, NY: Longman.

Murray, D. (1980). Writing as process: How writing finds its own meaning. In T. Donovan & B. McClelland (Eds.), *Eight approaches to teaching composition* (pp. 3–20). Urbana, IL: National Council of Teachers of English.

National Institute of Education. (1974). *Conference on studies in teaching: Teaching as a linguistic process in a cultural setting.* (ED 111 806)

Nelson, K. (1978). Children's thinking: What develops. In R. Siegler (Ed.), *How young children represent knowledge of their world in and out of language* (pp. 255–274). Hillsdale, NJ: Erlbaum.

Newell, G. (1984). Learning from writing in two content areas: A case study/protocol analysis. *Research in the Teaching of English, 18,* 265–285.

Newman, J. (1984). *The craft of children's writing.* Richmond Hill, ON: Scholastic.

North, S. (1987). *The making of knowledge in composition: Portrait of an emerging field.* Portsmouth, NH: Heinemann.

Odell, L., Cooper, C., & Courts, C. (1978). Discourse theory: Implications for research in composing. In C. Cooper & L. Odell (Eds.), *Research on composing: Points of departure* (pp. 1–12). Urbana, IL: National Council of Teachers of English.

Odell, L., Goswami, D., & Herrington, A. (1983). The discourse-based interview: A procedure for exploring the tacit knowledge of writers in nonacademic settings. In P. Mosenthal, L. Tamor, & S. Walmsley (Eds.), *Research on writing: Principles and methods* (pp. 220–235). White Plains, NY: Longman.

Ollila, L., & Mayfield, M. (Eds). (1992). *Emerging literacy: Preschool, kindergarten, and primary grades.* Needham Heights, MA: Allyn & Bacon.

Paivio, A., & Begg, I. (1981). *Psychology of language.* Englewood Cliffs, NJ: Prentice Hall.

Paris, S., & Cross, D. (1983). Ordinary learning: Pragmatic connections among children's beliefs, motives, and actions. In J. Bisanz, G. Bisanz, & R. Kail (Eds.), *Learning in children: Progress in cognitive development research* (pp. 137–163). New York: Springer-Verlag.

Perl, S. (1978). The composing processes of unskilled college writers. *Research in the Teaching of English, 13,* 317–336.

Pinnell, G.S., & Jagger, A. (1991). Oral language: Speaking and listening in the classroom. In J. Flood, J.M. Jensen, D. Lapp, & J.R. Squire (Eds.), *Handbook of research on teaching the English language arts* (pp. 691–720). New York: Macmillan.

Rasinski, T., & Deford, D. (1986). Students and their writing: Perceptions, motivations, and behaviours. In J. Niles & R. Lalik (Eds.), *Solving problems in literacy: Learners, teachers, and researchers* (pp. 294–299). Rochester, NY: National Reading Conference.

Resnick, L. (1991). Shared cognition: Thinking as social practice. In L. Resnick, J. Levine, & S. Teasley (Eds.), *Perspectives on socially shared cognition* (pp. 1–10). Washington, DC: American Psychological Association.

Scardamalia, M., & Bereiter, C. (1983). Child as coinvestigator: Helping children gain insight into their own mental processes. In S.G. Paris, G. Olson, & H. Stevenson (Eds.), *Learning and motivation in the classroom* (pp. 61–82). Hillsdale, NJ: Erlbaum.

Sinclair, J.M., & Brazil, D. (1982). *Teacher talk*. Oxford, UK: Oxford University Press.

Sinclair, J.M., & Coulthard, R. (1975). *Towards an analysis of discourse*. London: Oxford University Press.

Slobin, D. (Ed.). (1971). *The ontogenesis of grammar: A theoretical symposium*. New York: Academic.

Sommers, N. (1980). Revision strategies of student writers and experienced adult writers. *College Composition and Communication, 31,* 378–388.

Spradley, J. (1980). *Participant observation*. New York: Holt, Rinehart.

Stanovich, K. (1990). A call for an end to the paradigm wars in reading research. *Journal of Reading Behavior, 22*(3), 221–229.

Stein, N. (1986). Knowledge and process in the acquisition of writing skills. *Review of Research in Education, 13,* 225–258.

Strauss, A., & Corbin, J. (1990). *Basics of qualitative research: Grounded theory procedures and techniques*. Newbury Park, CA: Sage.

Strickland, D.S., & Cullinan, B.E. (1990). Afterword. In M.J. Adams, *Beginning to read: Thinking and learning about print* (pp. 426–433). Cambridge, MA: MIT Press.

Stubbs, M. (1976). *Language, schools and classrooms: Contemporary sociology of the school*. London: Methuen.

Stubbs, M., & Delamont, S. (1976). *Explorations in classroom observation*. New York: Wiley.

Tamor, L., & Bond, J. (1983). Text analysis: Inferring process from product. In P. Mosenthal, L. Tamor, & S. Walmsley (Eds.), *Research on writing: Principles and methods* (pp. 99–138). White Plains, NY: Longman.

Taylor, S., & Bogdan, R. (1984). *Introduction to qualitative research: The search for meanings* (2nd ed.). New York: Wiley.

Tierney, R.J. (1991). Studies of reading and writing growth: Longitudinal research on literacy development. In J. Flood, J.M. Jensen, D. Lapp, & J.R. Squire (Eds.), *Handbook of research on teaching the English language arts* (pp. 176–194). New York: Macmillan.

Tierney, R.J., Bridge, C., & Cera, M. (1979). The discourse processing operations of children. *Reading Research Quarterly, 4,* 541–569.

Tremmel, R. (1992). A habit of mind. *English Education, 24*(1), 20–33.

Vygotsky, L.S. (1934, 1962). *Thought and language*. Cambridge, MA: MIT Press.

Walker, R., & Adelman, C. (1976). Strawberries. In M. Stubbs & S. Delamont (Eds.), *Explorations in classroom observation*. New York: Wiley.

Wallace, B.A. (1989). *Choosing reality: A contemplative view of physics and the mind*. Boston, MA: New Science Library Shambhala.

Wells, G. (1986). *The meaning makers: Children learning language and using language to learn*. Portsmouth, NH: Heinemann.

Willes, M. (1983). *Children into pupils: A study of language in early schooling*. Boston, MA: Routledge & Kegan Paul.

Wixson, K., Bosky, A., Yochum, M., & Alvermann, D. (1984). An interview for assessing students' perceptions of classroom reading tasks. *The Reading Teacher, 37*(4), 346–352.

Young, R. (1978). Paradigms and problems: Needed research in rhetorical invention. In C. Cooper & L. Odell (Eds.), *Research on composing: Points of departure* (pp. 29–48). Urbana, IL: National Council of Teachers of English.

Zaharlick, A., & Green, J.L. (1991). Ethnographic research. In J. Flood, J.M. Jensen, D. Lapp, & J.R. Squire (Eds.), *Handbook of research on teaching the English language arts* (pp. 205–225). New York: Macmillan.

Author Index

Subject Index

Note: An "f" following an index entry indicates that the citation may be found in a figure.

STEVEN (STUDENT): interview, 15–16, 53, 70–71; writing sample, 58–59

STRATEGY INSTRUCTION, 29

STUDENT CONFERENCES, 30, 37–39

STUDENT INTERVIEWS, 15–16, 53, 64, 67, 70–71, 73–75; questions, 93–95

STUDENTS: number of pieces written by, 55–57, 56f; writing samples, 53–62

STUDENTS' PERCEPTIONS, 4, 63–79; of audience in writing, 71–73, 72f, 78; of author's expectations, 95; of goals and purposes of writing, 69–71, 70f, 77–78; of teacher's expectations, 94–95; of value of writing, 13, 74–77, 76f, 78; views of themselves as writers, 73–74, 74f, 78, 88; of what good writers do, 65–68, 66f, 77, 82–85; of what teachers do or say to help you be a better writer, 15–16, 67–68, 69f

SUSAN (STUDENT): journal writing, 1–2

T

TEACHER INTERVIEW QUESTIONS, 95–97

TEACHERS: instructional topics, 20, 20f; language of, 15–52; students' perceptions of, 15–16, 67–68, 69f; students' perceptions of expectations, 94–95. *See also* Pite, Norman

TEACHING: as crafting, 22. *See also* Writing instruction

THINK-ALOUD MODELING STRATEGIES, 89

THOUGHTS: writing to discover one's own, 49

TOMMY (STUDENT): journal writing, 1

TOOLS: for data collection, 93–100

TRANSACTIONAL WRITING, 10

U

UNDERSTANDING: definition of, 2; evident, 2

UNDERSTANDING OF WRITING: student interview questions, 94

V

VALUE OF WRITING, 13–14, 88–89; students' perceptions of, 13, 74–77, 76f, 78

W

WEBBING STRATEGY: example, 23

WRITERS: as first readers, 72; students' perceptions of what good ones do, 65–68, 66f, 77, 82–85; students' views of themselves as, 73–74, 74f, 78, 88

WRITING: assessment of, 84–85; attitudes toward, 94; audience in, 11–12, 36–41, 42f, 71–73, 72f, 78, 86–88; children's perceptions of, 97; for communicating through a particular form, 47; as crafting, 22; for discovery, 43, 49; effective elements, 9–14; for enjoyment, 46–47; examples of, 57–62; expressive, 10, 13, 88; functions of, 10; goals and purposes of, 10, 41–51, 51f, 69–71, 70f, 77–78, 85–86; journal, 1–2; kinds of, 54–57, 55f; learning, 81; number of pieces written by Norman's students, 55–57, 56f; for personal expression, 44–45; poetic, 10; for practice, 50; presentation of, 39; reflective accounts, 4, 64; rehearsal for, 9; to remember or explain, 48–49; to share one's work with others, 50; think-aloud modeling strategies, 89; transactional, 10; types of, 10; understanding of, 94; value of, 13–14, 74–78, 88–89; what good writers do, 65–68, 77, 82–85; what is important for, 83; writing to share one's, 50